Editor-in-Chief and Founder:
Lyndon H. LaRouche, Jr.
Editorial Board: *Lyndon H. LaRouche, Jr. , Helga Zepp-LaRouche, Paul Gallagher, Tony Papert, Gerald Rose, Dennis Small, Jeffrey Steinberg, William Wertz*
Co-Editors: *Paul Gallagher, Tony Papert*
Managing Editor: *Nancy Spannaus*
Technology: *Marsha Freeman*
Books: *Katherine Notley*
Ebooks: *Richard Burden*
Graphics: *Alan Yue*
Photos: *Stuart Lewis*
Circulation Manager: *Stanley Ezrol*

INTELLIGENCE DIRECTORS
Counterintelligence: *Jeffrey Steinberg, Michele Steinberg*
Economics: *John Hoefle, Marcia Merry Baker, Paul Gallagher*
History: *Anton Chaitkin*
Ibero-America: *Dennis Small*
Russia and Eastern Europe: *Rachel Douglas*
United States: *Debra Freeman*

INTERNATIONAL BUREAUS
Bogotá: *Miriam Redondo*
Berlin: *Rainer Apel*
Copenhagen: *Tom Gillesberg*
Houston: *Harley Schlanger*
Lima: *Sara Madueño*
Melbourne: *Robert Barwick*
Mexico City: *Gerardo Castilleja Chávez*
New Delhi: *Ramtanu Maitra*
Paris: *Christine Bierre*
Stockholm: *Ulf Sandmark*
United Nations, N.Y.C.: *Leni Rubinstein*
Washington, D.C.: *William Jones*
Wiesbaden: *Göran Haglund*

ON THE WEB
e-mail: eirns@larouchepub.com
www.larouchepub.com
www.executiveintelligencereview.com
www.larouchepub.com/eiw
Webmaster: *John Sigerson*
Assistant Webmaster: *George Hollis*
Editor, Arabic-language edition: *Hussein Askary*

EIR (ISSN 0273-6314) *is published weekly (50 issues), by EIR News Service, Inc., P.O. Box 17390, Washington, D.C. 20041-0390. (703) 777-9451*

European Headquarters: E.I.R. GmbH, Postfach Bahnstrasse 9a, D-65205, Wiesbaden, Germany
Tel: 49-611-73650
Homepage: http://www.eirna.com
e-mail: eirna@eirna.com
Director: Georg Neudecker

Montreal, Canada: 514-461-1557

Denmark: EIR - Danmark, Sankt Knuds Vej 11, basement left, DK-1903 Frederiksberg, Denmark. Tel.: +45 35 43 60 40, Fax: +45 35 43 87 57. e-mail: eirdk@hotmail.com.

Mexico City: EIR, Sor Juana Inés de la Cruz 242-2 Col. Agricultura C.P. 11360 Delegación M. Hidalgo, México D.F. Tel. (5525) 5318-2301 eirmexico@gmail.com

Are You a Dupe Of Satan?

The Encyclical from Hell

by Paul Gallagher

June 22—Anyone who reads the encyclical written by Commander of the Order of the British Empire John Schellnhuber for issuance by Pope Francis, cannot escape its call for the destruction of mankind—that sinful and violent race made from the mere soil of the creator "Mother Earth."

Pope Francis presumably does not want to wipe out most of the human species. But the British Royal Family does—publicly so—and the Pope has capitulated to the leading Satanic forces on Earth. The Encyclical *Laudato Si'* is a horrible corruption of the Catholic Church and of Christianity. It is also an assault against science, technological progress, and the idea of human beings as co-creators with the Creator.

The fact that the Pope of 1.2 billion Catholics—the Vatican which has blocked international "climate conferences" from issuing the British royals' Malthusian global edicts—has been roped into issuing and promoting *Laudato Si'*, represents a threat to human civilization of the most serious nature.

The controlling author of the Encyclical was Hans Joachim "John" Schellnhuber of Oxford, who states that the maximum number of human beings which can be sustained by "Mother Earth" is "less than 1 billion." He is momentarily and violently trying to deny these statements, but they were made at international climate conferences and reported in major press.

The British royals, and their other leading anti-science agents such as Martin Palmer and Sir David Attenborough, shamelessly state that the human race is a pollution of Mother Earth—its growth is the root of all evils and problems, according to Sir David—and should be leveled, by any means necessary, to "less than 1 billion" in number. *Laudato Si'* author Schellnhuber has been a personal agent deployed by and with Queen Elizabeth and Prince Charles since at least 2004, to demand that major governments agree to "decarbonize" and scrap modern industry.

Prometheus Again Bound

From the opening words of *Laudato Si'*, this Encyclical stands opposed to all others dealing with social matters by the Popes since Leo XIII. Whereas those encyclicals always put the human being "in the center" as most beloved of the Creator, this one pictures mankind as the great polluter, if not pollution itself.

Pollution, moreover, of a different creator, called "Mother Earth."

"Praise be to you, my Lord, through our Sister, Mother Earth, who sustains and governs us, and who produces various fruit with coloured flowers and herbs," the Encyclical opens [as translated to English on the site of the Holy See].

"2. This sister now cries out to us because of the harm we have inflicted on her by our irresponsible use and abuse of the goods with which God has endowed her. We have come to see ourselves as her lords and masters [having been given "dominion" over her, is a better translation of the original into English—ed.], entitled to plunder her at will. The violence present in our hearts, wounded by sin, is also reflected in the symptoms of sickness evident in the soil, in the water, in the air and in all forms of life. This is why the Earth herself, burdened and laid waste, is among the most abandoned and maltreated of our poor; she 'groans in travail' (Rom 8:22). We have forgotten that we ourselves are dust of the earth (cf. Gen 2:7); our very bodies are made up of her elements, we breathe her air and we receive life and refreshment from her waters."

The worship of Mother Earth as creator, is paganism, including its Satanist forms. This rejects both the scientific view of mankind's activity, and the Christian one—*Genesis* itself.

> "Inasmuch as we all generate small ecological damage, we are called to acknowledge our contribution, smaller or greater, to the disfigurement and destruction of creation."

Did the ancient Greeks disfigure and destroy the shore on which they built Athens, or the sea on which they sailed? Did Kepler disfigure and destroy the Solar System by discovering God's design of it? Astronauts by exploring it? Do our spacecraft destroy the Earth by mapping and measuring it? Did oil disfigure the smoky wood-burning society which preceded it, or the discoverers of nuclear isotopes disfigure and destroy medical patients? How many of those "flowers and fruits" were created in the biosphere by the human species?

Despite covering itself in passing quotes from every conceivable previous Papal document, this one is their opposite. Compare what Schellnhuber et al. quote from Saint John Paul II's *Redemptor Hominis*:

> Authentic human development has a moral character. It presumes full respect for the human person, but it must also be concerned for the world around us and take into account the nature of each being and of its mutual connection in an ordered system.[8] Accordingly, our human ability to transform reality must proceed in line with God's original gift of all that is;

with what Schellnhuber et al. wrote for Pope Francis in *Laudato Si'*:

> We must be grateful for the praiseworthy efforts being made by scientists and engineers dedicated to finding solutions to *man-made* problems [emphasis added]. But a sober look at our world shows that the degree of human intervention is actually making our earth less rich and beautiful, ever more limited and grey, even as technological advances and consumer goods continue to abound limitlessly. We seem to think that we can substitute an irreplaceable and irretrievable beauty with something which we have created ourselves.

The Encyclical plods through the most superficial two- to three-paragraph glosses on forms of "pollution"; almost appealing to the sub-teenaged "pollution—eeuuw, gross!" without attempting any scientific or engineering depth, possible advances, or possible solutions.

Some might try to excuse this, reciting, "The Pope is not an economist." But *Laudato Si'* is Malthusian economics, of the most evil kind. It would again take from mankind the Promethean fire of technology, and push humanity down to the wretched state from which Prometheus rescued it.

The encyclical declares Promethean foresight "wrong."

> An inadequate presentation of Christian anthropology gave rise to a wrong understanding of the relationship between human beings and the world. Often, what was handed on was a Promethean vision of mastery over the world....

The paragraph dismisses "the human being in the center"—anthropocentrism is "misguided."

Most criminally, it declares that progress is a "myth," and it effectively denies that scientific and technological progress can uplift the poor, making this British encyclical from Hell a direct attack on the developing nations first of all.

Resistance

Through this Encyclical, the British Royals have laid claim to control of the Roman Catholic Church with its 1.2 billion adherents.

They showed off their control of the U.S. President with a shameless "BBC America" program June 28 in which Obama brought genocidalist David Attenborough to the Oval Office, played BBC interviewer for him, lavishly praised Attenborough, and agreed to his statements that population growth is the world's most serious problem.

Thus, the royals can now give the "go" signal to their puppet Obama, to solve the overpopulation problem within a few hours by triggering his confrontations with China and Russia into actual thermonuclear war.

If you believe in the future of our unique human species—on this planet and in the Solar System and the galaxy—you must mobilize yourself now to save humanity from the threat represented by this encyclical.

EIR Contents

www.larouchepub.com   Volume 42, Number 27, July 3, 2015

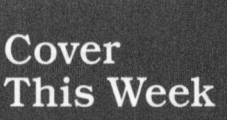

Cover This Week

Hans Joachim 'John' Schellnhuber

Potsdam Institute for Climate Impact Research

John Satanhuber, author of the so-called Papal Encyclical Laudate Si'.

Note to Subscribers: *EIR* will not produce the issue which would come out on July 10. The next issue after July 3, will be dated July 17.

We Are All Greeks! Europe Only Has a Future With the New Silk Road

by Helga Zepp-LaRouche

Helga Zepp-LaRouche is founder of the Schiller Institutes, President of the German Schiller Institute, and Chairwoman of the BüSo political party in Germany.

June 28—Dear Citizens!

It's not Greece which has failed, but rather Chancellor Angela Merkel, Finance Minister Wolfgang Schäuble, the EU Commission, the European Central Bank, and the IMF. Why should the Greek government stick with the austerity measures demanded by the European Union (EU), which have already reduced the Greek economy by a third, lowered the birth rate, raised the death rate, and increased youth unemployment to 65%? A policy that even the IMF had to admit was completely incompetent, and that the UN expert on debt and human rights condemned as a clear violation of human rights? Greek Prime Minister Alexis Tsipras's decision not to capitulate to the "shock and awe" method of the Eurogroup's Shylocks is not only correct, but offers the chance for all of Europe to break with the insanity of the casino economy, which only serves the interests of the banks and speculators—provided, however, that Germany and other countries find the courage to mobilize Europe's moral and intellectual strengths.

If panic now breaks out on the financial markets and the European economy collapses, Greece will not be to blame, but rather the fact that the entire trans-Atlantic system is hopelessly bankrupt. Instead of using the threatened meltdown around the bankruptcy of Lehman Brothers and AIG in September 2008 to regulate the banking system and to ban speculative excesses, a gigantic redistribution took place, transforming private gambling debts into public debts, and the taxpayers had to pay for the bailouts. In the case of Greece, only 3% of the bailout funds stayed in the country, while the rest flowed back into the European banks, allowing the speculators to dance even more wildly around the Golden Calf. The reality is that the trans-Atlantic banks, which are supposedly "too big to fail," are 40% larger today than they were in 2008, and the total of derivatives amounts to something approaching $2 quadrillion. And that is exactly what could disappear into thin air in an uncontrollable crash, in a "Grexit" [exit of Greece from the Eurozone—ed.].

Just in time for the explosion of the crisis, the Bank for International Settlements (BIS) announced in its annual report that the world has no defense for the next financial crisis, since the central banks have already fired off all their ammunition. They even outmaneuvered themselves, since with their repeated interest rate cuts, they created all the preconditions for the next crash. In fact: "The game is over, Mr Schäuble—but not for Greece, but for your own failed policies!"

That is precisely why the Greek government's demand for a debt conference—not only for Greece, but for all of Europe—is absolutely on the mark. A drastic debt "haircut," in tandem with the introduction of a Glass-Steagall two-tier banking system on both sides of the Atlantic, must put an end to the casino economy. In its place, we need to establish a credit system, similar, for example, to the Kreditanstalt für Wiederaufbau [Reconstruction Finance Agency], which was created after World War II to finance the real economy, generating the German "economic miracle." Without such a fundamental reorganization of the financial system—i.e., continuing with "bailouts" or "bail-ins" ad nauseam (the Cyprus blueprint of Eurogroup head Jeroen Dijsselbloem)—the impact on the savings of every citizen in Europe and the United States will be very much worse than what the Greek population is enduring today. Solidarity with Greece is the best thing you can do for yourself and for your own future!

There is a very real and immediate way out of this crisis: The "win-win" strategy offered by China—i.e., cooperation to build the New Silk Road, the so-called "One Road, One Belt" policy, which President Xi Jinping proposed at the APEC summit in Beijing last November to President Obama and the heads of other major countries—provides a real prospect for overcoming the evil of geopolitics. In the West, China's New Silk Road policy was virtually ignored for nearly two years; now the realization is belatedly dawning, that this revival of the ancient Silk Road has picked up incredibly impressive momentum. It represents a dynamic that one could only describe as "A Grand Design in Action."

Along with the Asian Infrastructure Investment Bank (AIIB) and the new financial institutions of the BRICS countries [Brazil, Russia, India, China, South Africa], a parallel economic and financial system has evolved in the last two years, based on exactly the same economic principles as the American System of Alexander Hamilton, Friedrich List, Otto von Bismarck, and the German economic miracle in the post-war period.

The EU-China Summit on June 29 could be the beginning of such cooperation. China has already expressed its interest in generous investments in European infrastructure projects, and European Commission President Jean-Claude Juncker announced that the €315 billion investment plan of the European Fund for Strategic Investments (EFSI) so far has no investors to provide a real capital line for it. In its preparations for the summit, China expressed great interest in cooperating with this Fund for the implementation of the New Silk Road.

Thus, the 2012 program of the BüSo [Civil Rights Solidarity Movement—ed.] for extending the New Silk Road to Southern Europe and the Mediterranean is coming immediately within reach. Greece can—along with the Balkans, Italy, Spain, and Portugal—very soon experience the same economic development that China's economic miracle has demonstrated over the last 30 years. Prime Minister Tsipras has, with his recent trips to Russia and China, already had extensive conversations about how Greece, which has had long historical and deep cultural ties with both nations, can cooperate with the New Silk Road and the BRICS countries and become part of the new dynamic. Europe should take up Greece's offer to be a bridge between Europe and the BRICS.

However, if the EU responds to the generous Chinese offer by trying to subvert the new Chinese institutions with the old neo-liberal monetarist and failed concepts or with the satanic climate swindle of Commander of the British Empire Hans Joachim Schellnhuber, as it just appeared in the new Encyclical of Pope Francis, then this will mean, in all likelihood, missing the last chance to save the world before the crash.

Germany Can Prevent World War

Germany is the country which can actually do something to overcome the acute danger of war. If Germany declares that it is lifting the sanctions against Russia, all the major states in Europe will do the same thing. Such a decisive move to prevent continental European confrontation against Russia would improve the strategic situation on the spot, and strengthen the forces in the United States that want to bring that country's Constitution back into force.

The argument that Germany can do nothing because it is an occupied country, is absurd. If the choice is whether we, as a target in a nuclear war, want to be wiped out—and that is exactly the threat we face, if we do not oppose the geopolitical confrontation against Russia and China—or whether we want to pursue our interest in survival, then it should be possible to muster the political will for the second option. And if Frau Merkel and Herr Schäuble cannot come to this realization, then ways and means must be urgently found to replace them with people who are serious about the general welfare of the German people.

The way out of this existential crisis, which can lead to the extinction of the human species in a global thermonuclear war, lies in overcoming the geopolitics that already led to two world wars in the Twentieth Century. Former Chancellor Helmut Schmidt is right that the cause of the Ukraine crisis lies in the policy of the EU since it was created by the Maastricht Treaty in 1992, which precisely began the geopolitical expansion eastward, up to the borders of Russia. Not only the euro, but also the imperial EU, is a failed experiment that we need to end as soon as possible. As a Europe of the Fatherlands [sovereign nations—ed.], which is united by the joint mission of cooperation with the New Silk Road for global development, we will be stronger together than ever was the case in the EU of Maastricht.

We should accept Xi Jinping's offer for cooperation with the New Silk Road, in a "win-win" strategy for all the world's nations. We need a completely new paradigm of thinking, oriented to the common interests of mankind.

The way out of this existential crisis is open, and the good news is that there is a clear solution. Whether this opportunity is seized depends upon us all. You all, every single one of you, can contribute to bringing it about!

Translated from German by EIR's Leesburg and Wiesbaden bureaus.

The British Royal Family's Plan To Return the World to the Stone Age

by Michael Billington

June 28—No wonder British Royal Family and its stable of genocidalists have rushed to praise the new Papal Encyclical *Laudato Si'*. It was largely written by their own long-time lackey Hans-Joachim (John) Schellnhuber, who was appointed Commander of the Order of the British Empire by Queen Elizabeth in 2004. With this Encyclical, the British Monarchy claims to have captured the Vatican as a tool of their long-standing campaign to reduce world population to about one billion, driving the world back into stone-age conditions, without fossil fuels or nuclear power. In fact, their hoisting the House of Windsor flag over St. Peter's Basilica, should serve as a warning that they are about to instruct Barack Obama, their asset in the White House, to proceed with his thermonuclear war against Russia and China, a war which is already in the final stages of preparation.

His Royal Virus, Consort to the Queen of England, Prince Philip. A 2007 photograph.

The Encyclical claiming the capture of the Vatican, is the culmination of a thirty-year campaign by the Queen's Consort, Prince Philip,—famous for his desire to be reincarnated as a deadly virus in order to help solve the "overpopulation problem." His scheme was to seize control over major world religions, to then use them as a battering-ram to destroy the fruit of the hated Italian Renaissance: science, technology, industry, and republican government. This would complete the work left unfinished by 150 years of religious warfare in Europe after 1492.

1986 was the 25th Anniversary of the founding of the World Wildlife Fund, which had been co-founded by Philip and Prince Bernhard of the Netherlands, a card-carrying member of the Nazi Party. On that occasion, Philip sponsored a conference in Assisi, Italy, to create the "WWF Religion and Conservation Network." It aimed at degrading the world's religions, injecting into them all an animist, pagan worship of "Mother Earth," and launching them into a satanic attack on science, technology and population growth as "destructive of the environment." The intent was to destroy the social and cultural capacity of nations to resist British Empire genocide.

This evil political purpose is exemplified by the fact that the person placed in charge of this operation by Prince Philip, one Martin Palmer, is also the British Empire's leading intelligence agent in their effort to subvert China.

Back to 'Nature Faiths'

Palmer, Philip's "religious advisor," ran the WWF Religion and Conservation Network, which morphed into the Alliance for Religion and Conservation (ARC) in 1995 at a conference held in Windsor Castle. And just last week, the ARC issued a statement hailing Pope Francis's climate change Encyclical as "something very extraordinary in the journey to link religions with conservation and conservation with religions."

Palmer wrote in his 1992 book *Coming of Age: An Exploration of Christianity and the New Age*, that Christianity was guilty of the "deification of humanity and its products, science and industry." Prince Philip, at the 1995 founding of ARC, attended by representatives of nine world religions, called for "vital action" to protect the environment from

ARC/Katia Marsh
Prince Philip (right) with the Secretary General of his Alliance of Religion and Conservation, Martin Palmer.

the dramatic increase in the world's human population. The key issue for the conservation of our natural environment is to find ways of protecting it from the consequences of the human population explosion.

In an interview with an investigative journalist in 1986 about the purpose of that Assisi conference, Palmer gushed:

> The whole idea for these Assisi events came from Prince Philip personally, once he realized that there existed other ways of viewing the relationship between man and nature, than just the Western way. The word from Prince Philip is that, after this week, world religions can never remain the same.

The idea was to degrade the great religions, especially Christianity itself, to the same status as what Palmer called "nature faiths," referring to aboriginal animist religions and Taoism, which view man as co-equal to the animals and to primitive nature. The Assisi conference would launch

> alternative ways of perceiving nature, where we, the human race, are not the kingpins who can destroy as much as we wish. What we do is, we look more at the Chinese attitude toward the

land, the notion that life is cyclical, not linear, that humanity is *not* the end of creation.

Palmer elaborated the point in response to a question on the implications of the Gaia hypothesis:

> What the earth cares about is its own continued survival, and if this means shrugging off humanity, then so be it. One of the most challenging ideas emerging from the environmental crisis and from concepts such as Gaia, is the notion that humanity really isn't that important. This poses major problems to Christianity, Judaism, and Islam ....

This was nearly 30 years ago. Now, the fact that Prince Philip's Commander of the British Empire, John Schellnhuber, has now trumpeted the capture the Vatican for this anti-Christian, anti-human view of the world, must be recognized as the enormous threat that it is. Even then, In 1986, Palmer bragged that he had "good working relations" with leading figures in the Vatican and the Justice and Peace (Justitia et Pax) group. The current head of the Justitia et Pax, Cardinal Turkson, is a rabid environmentalist, and participated along with Schellnhuber at the official release of the climate change Encyclical.

Targets: Christianity and Confucianism

In addition to his duties in service of Prince Philip's efforts to eliminate six of every seven human beings, Palmer is also one of the United Kingdom's leading China scholars. His work in China is totally consistent with his promotion of Satanic, anti-human environmentalist ideology. Palmer glorifies Taoism (Daoism) over Confucianism as the core of "Chinese thought."

Some of the 400 Taoist deities in a temple area designated for praying and meditation.

Although professing to be a Christian, Palmer is actually a Satanist, violently opposed to the Christian concept of *imago viva dei*, that man is created in the living image of God, through the creative power of the mind to discover and apply the laws of the universe, making it possible for Mankind to follow the mandate in Genesis to "have dominion" over nature. In an interview with *China Daily* on April 24, 2015, Palmer said that when he first visited a Taoist temple in China, he was "fascinated and challenged" by the existence of over 400 gods, and that being able to pray not to One God but to many, was "delightfully liberating" to him.

Palmer added:

My Christianity is deeply shaped by my Taoism. I was only able to become a Christian because understanding Taoism helped me throw away some of the baggage of Christianity.

To Palmer, that "baggage" referred to the concept of *imago viva dei*, and the Genesis command for man to bring dominion over nature, and to "be fruitful, and multiply, and replenish the earth, and subdue it."

This is the man Prince Philip has entrusted to subvert China, which is currently leading the world towards a new world economic order, through the New Silk Road process unleashed by President Xi Jinping, and the BRICS alliance based on global development and new international financial institutions, as an alternative to the bankrupt trans-Atlantic system.

In an interview with the Pulitzer Center on October 23, 2014, Palmer said:

How on earth do you stop this juggernaut, thundering forward, of industrialization, of pollution, of commercialization of consumerism? You look for the alternatives, and you begin to promote those alternatives. The alternative, in every culture, is a simpler lifestyle inspired by deeper values.

In China, this means, for Palmer, the Taoist tradition, rather than the Confucian tradition. He has made his name as a translator of the Taoist texts,—the *Tao Te Ching* of Lao Tzu and the writings of Chuang Tzu. Perhaps the best example of the opposite approaches to science and technology taken by the Confucians and the Taoists, is the famous passage from the Taoist Chuang Tzu, who imagines a meeting between a disciple of Confucius and a Taoist peasant who is scooping water with a cup to irrigate his field.

The Confucian says: "If you had a machine here, in a day you could irrigate one hundred times your present area. The labor required is trifling as compared with the work done. Would you not like one?" He describes a well-sweep, whose foot-driven pulley with wooden scoops lifts water from an irrigation ditch.

The Taoist peasant denounces him, insisting that anyone who is cunning with instruments must also have a scheming heart, cannot be pure and incorrupt, and is thus not a fit vehicle for the Tao (the "Way"). "It is not that I do not know of such things," he says, "but I should be ashamed to use them." (Chuang Tzu, 12).

Thus, Taoism corresponds to the Satanic current in the West which degrades man to an animal, fit only for manual labor and bare subsistence (except for the oligarchs, of course).

The Role of Joseph Needham

There is a history to the fact that Palmer holds his position as the leading China expert in the UK, beloved by the Royal Family. In the *China Daily* interview mentioned above, Palmer acknowledges that he was trained directly by Joseph Needham, the British Empire's preeminent profiler and saboteur of

creative commons

The Taoist ideal of labor, being carried out in a field in North Korea.

China's development until his death in 1995 at the age of 95. Palmer studied under Needham at Cambridge from 1973-75, with an emphasis on China Studies and theology.

Needham, as *EIR* has <u>documented</u> (see "Obituary: The Taoist Hell of Joseph Needham, 1900-1995" by Michael Billington, *EIR*, April 21, 1995), began his career as a biochemist in the circles of geneticist J.B.S. Haldane, Bertrand Russell, and Julian Huxley. Needham collaborated with Huxley in the creation of UNESCO, which from the outset was an occult-infested British intelligence nest within the United Nations Organization, and was directly involved in the creation of Prince Philip's WWF. In his 16-volume *Science and Civilization in China*, Needham compiled many facts regarding Chinese scientific discoveries in the era preceding the European Renaissance, but credits those discoveries to Taoism and the belief in magic. As I wrote in the obituary:

> Needham acknowledged that the Confucian tradition was that of rational thought, based on the concept of man as fundamentally good, endowed by Heaven with certain virtues, the foremost being the love of truth (*ren*), whereas the opposite, Taoist tradition was one of mysticism, magic, and the belief that man is no more meaningful in the cosmic reality than a rock or a worm. And yet, Needham held Confucianism re-

sponsible for the retardation of science in China, while the great scientific developments of the earlier ages were credited to the alchemy of the Taoists!

"Rational theology," he wrote, "was anti-scientific, mystical theology proved to be pro-scientific." Taoists, he claimed, like the alchemists in the West, launched "real science" through the empiricist, directionless mixing of chemicals in search of magic potions.

Nor was Needham's embrace of Taoism based simply on its rejection of science. He declared his favorite passage from the *Tao Te Ching* of Lao Tzu to be:

> Heaven and Earth are without benevolence.
> They treat the 10,000 things as straw dogs.
> Nor is the Sage benevolent.
> To him also are the hundred clans but straw dogs.

The Chinese word for "benevolence" here is *ren*, which in Confucianism has a connotation similar to *agape* in Christianity, referring to the love of God and Mankind as a whole. The intention of Taoism, and of Palmer and Needham, is clear. Like Zeus and the gods of Olympus, they insist that Mankind be treated like an animal, through punishment and reward, and access to technology must be denied him. Zeus condemned Prometheus to perpetual torture for the crime of providing the knowledge of fire to the human race.

In the 1986 interview with an investigative journalist referenced above, Needham's protégé Palmer even argued that trees should not be cut down, since a tree "has the same right to exist as man." He identified the enemy of Prince Philip's WWF as "the ideas of the last 200 years," pointing explicitly to the American Revolution.

"The real problem," Palmer said, "is the industrialization matrix of philosophy and thought," identifying four historical trends as causes for this "industrial matrix," which he insists must be reversed. These include:

• the era of Bismarck in creating the German sovereign state;

• the evolution of Catholic Humanism under Leonardo da Vinci and Erasmus during the Christian Renaissance;

• the rediscovery of Greek Platonism after the fall of Constantinople in 1453 (a reference to the work of Nicholas of Cusa, whose scientific and philosophical ideas launched the Renaissance); and

• the creation of the United States, noting that this was the confluence of the first three.

These are, of course, the key processes in modern history which pulled humanity out of several dark ages, allowing the vast expansion of populations at higher standards of living and with longer life spans.

Today, as these processes are indeed being destroyed in the Western world under the domination of the British financial Empire, China is becoming still more important as a target for the Satanists.

The 2009 UN Climate Change Conference in Copenhagen, which the British Empire intended to be the launching of a global genocide policy under the guise of mandatory carbon reductions worldwide,—ostensibly to stop (non-existent) global warming,—totally failed, due to strong resistance from China and India, which recognized that such restrictions would cripple their efforts to escape from poverty and backwardness through industrial and scientific development. This November, in Paris, the 2015 UN Climate Change Conference will begin.

The British Empire claims that they will be able to reverse the failure of 2009, and impose a global, mandatory restriction on so-called "greenhouse gases." For this to be realized, China (and India) must be reined in. This is where Palmer's profiling and psychological warfare against the Confucian tradition come into play.

Palmer himself is playing an active role in the current drive. A July 21 Paris "Summit of Conscience for Climate," to be hosted by the French government, was Palmer's idea. That summit will see a specially invited audience of 300 "religious and moral figures" sit around for a day listening to each other speak on "why I care" about the climate—as part of the buildup for the official meetings in the fall.

Two Paradigms

The world is increasingly aware that there are now two totally distinct paradigms at play in the world. On the one hand, the collapsing trans-Atlantic world, imposing austerity upon their own nations to salvage bankrupt financial institutions, waging perpetual war across the globe and threatening thermonuclear war on Russia and China, while internally decaying socially under the domination of the now-predominant rock-drug-sex counter-culture.

But there is another system coming into being, centered on China's New Silk Road initiatives, the emergence of the BRICS alliance, and the new financial institutions coming into being this year and next, to finance great infrastructure projects throughout the developing sector nations.

This latter is seen as the enemy of the British Empire and its stooge Obama. Just as Joseph Needham subverted China, even offering full support for the bestial "Cultural Revolution" in 1966-75, especially for the "Anti-Confucius Campaign" during the Cultural Revolution,—so also is Martin Palmer the Royal Family's hitman against China's renewed Confucian role in the world under President Xi Jinping, based on the harmony of interests among all people through development. Palmer does not hide his intentions. In the Pulitzer Center interview referenced above, he calls for the overthrow of the Chinese Government. Palmer "predicts" that the "Chinese Communist Party may very well be one of the shorter-lived dynasties in history," because the "relationship between religion [i.e., Taoism—ed.] and politics will come to a burning point within the next 20-30 years. In Xinjiang and Tibet you could argue it already has."

Palmer and Prince Philip actually have a far shorter time frame in mind,—as short as a few weeks.

Crucial background for this report came from two articles by Mark Burdman published in EIR *in 1986 (*"Prince Philip to Set a New 'Satanist Covenant' in Assisi"*) and 1996 (*"Martin Palmer, Prince Philip's Guru"*).*

How the British Crown Reduced Ireland's 'Carrying Capacity' to 6 Million Souls

by Paul Gallagher

It is, unfortunately, a well-known fact that today's population of Ireland, about six million including both the Republic and Ulster, is less, by two million, than its population of two centuries ago. While Europe's population as a whole became 4.5 times greater over those two centuries, that one small part of Europe under near-continuous British Crown financial and political domination all that time, has lost a quarter of its population.

This is what the British royal family wishes, by the public statements of its members today, for the whole world. Queen Elizabeth, Prince Philip, Prince Charles, and their scholarly retinue claim that the "carrying capacity" of old Mother Earth is—*and therefore the world population should be, in the future*—some 1-2 billion people, not 7.2 billion as it is today.

How did the British Crown impose its wish upon Ireland?

Beginning 170 years ago this Fall, British Crown policy caused the genocide of two million out of eight million Irish subjects in four years. In contrast to the Nazis, the British perpetrators of this 1845-1849 genocide were not punished for their policies, nor did they change them in any way afterwards.

In their quoted statements on that episode

Prime responsibility for starving the Irish people lay with Queen Victoria (r. 1837-1901), shown here in 1887, and her Prime Minister Lord John Russell, who was in office from 1846 to 1852.

of genocide, presented below, you will recognize precisely the view of Prince Philip "Deadly Virus" Windsor today, regarding reducing the population—pollution, in his view—of "common" people in the world.

Not Potatoes, But Debt Slavery

Any historian who has studied the subject knows that potatoes (or the lack thereof) did not cause the Irish famine and genocide 170 years ago. The potato blight which struck the harvest in Autumn 1845, had begun in

North Carolina, and spread to destroy potato crops throughout the Northern Hemisphere for several years; but it did not cause famine or mass death anywhere except in Ireland.

Nor were potatoes the only major produce of Irish agriculture at the time; they were just the only produce which the Irish—75% of whom had become tenants of British landlords—were allowed to eat or to feed to their livestock. The historian Arthur Young had written in 1841 that in the course of two generations to that point, Irish tenant farmers had become slaves in effect:

Clothing being distributed during the Irish Potato Famine.

A landlord in Ireland can scarcely invent an order which a laborer, servant, or cottier [tenant farmer] dares to refuse .... He may punish with his cane or his horsewhip with the most perfect security. A poor man would have his bones broken if he offered to lift a hand in his own defense.

British traders exported or sold all the corn, wheat, barley, and oats Irish farmers grew, in order that they should pay their rents. All crops became cash crops—and there was nothing left for the farmer and his family to eat. While a million Irish starved to death, the British Crown heavily deployed troops to protect the export ships. All farmers who stopped paying their rents were instantly evicted, and the large landlords, led by then-British Foreign Minister Lord Palmerston, evicted their tenants more rapidly than before as they were starving in the 1840s, even evicting many who were still paying rent. Free trade decreed that no money would be spent for employment on infrastructure projects such as drainage, harbors, fisheries, etc., though a committee of prominent Irish subjects led by Thomas Drummond had quickly surveyed what was most needed. Ireland at that time had 164 miles of railways; England had 6,621 miles.

No government surplus food was available to the starving. The destitute were put on the road works or in the workhouses by the hundreds of thousands, received almost no net wages after their debts and rents were collected, and died in large numbers "on the works" and in the Poor Law houses.

The Irish population was 8.2-8.4 million in 1845. Some 1.5 million human beings died of starvation and disease in Ireland in four years, while more than one million attempted to emigrate; of these, about 500,000 died—usually of typhus—in the Atlantic passage or in quarantine camps in Canada and New England. The Montreal Board of Health stated of those in the camps in 1847, "It may well be supposed that few of the survivors could reach any other than an early grave." In that period, among the Irish emigrant population of Massachusetts, average life expectancy was estimated by Lemuel Shattuck at 13.4 years, with 60% dying by the age of 5: a level characteristic of Stone Age human societies.

When it was "over," the British officials directly in charge of "Irish famine relief," particularly acting Treasury Minister Sir Charles Trevelyan, congratulated themselves and were decorated when Queen Victoria made her gala 1848 visit to and "progress" through Ireland. As 1847 ended, Trevelyan wrote:

It is my opinion that too much has been done for the people. Under such treatment the people have grown worse instead of better, and we must now try what independent exertion, and the operation of natural causes, can do.... I shall rest after two years of such continuous hard work in public service, as I have never had in my life.

Then, having vacationed in France, he added:

[The] problem of Irish overpopulation being altogether beyond the power of man, the cure had been supplied by the direct stroke of an all-wise Providence.

Ireland's population continued to fall after 1850, though more slowly, reaching a low of just over four million by the early Twentieth Century.

The British historian Charles Kingsley, who accompanied the Queen on her gracious and glorious visit, wrote:

I am daunted by the human chimpanzees I saw along that 100 miles of horrible country. I don't believe they are our fault. I believe that there are not only many more of them than of old, but that they are happier, better and more comfortably fed and lodged under our rule than they ever were. But to see white chimpanzees is dreadful; if they were black, one would not feel it so much.

However, Lord Clarendon, the British viceroy in Ireland during the famine, saw the situation more clearly. He wrote to Prime Minister Lord John Russell:

I don't think there is another legislature in Europe [other than the British] that would coldly persist in this policy of extermination.

How It Was Done

British Crown policy had been working to create this disaster for a long time previously. The crucial period was the 1785-1845 policies of William Petty, the second Lord Shelburne, and Prime Minister William Pitt, who took over the British governments after the American Revolution, and for whom Adam Smith

wrote his *Wealth of Nations* and other "free trade" tracts.

The great Irish writer and leader Jonathan Swift had written already in 1730:

One-half of all Irish rents is spent in England ... with other incidents, (it) will amount to full half of the income of the whole kingdom, all clear profit to England.... The rise of our rents is squeezed out of the very blood, and vitals, and clothes, and dwellings of the tenants, who live worse than English beggars.

However, during that Eighteenth Century the condition of the Irish had improved for the first time since the Cromwellian invasion in 1653 (which also explicitly intended genocide, though failing to achieve it). This improvement was due in large part to the organizing efforts of Swift and his Leibnizian networks.

In particular, the Irish merchant marine had been revived, her ports improved, effective taxes lowered, and the clothing, linen, and glass industries developed, and agriculture had been improved. The Penal Laws of the 1690s had been intended to insure that Irish Catholics would be reduced to potato culture on land rented from British landlords. But effective organizing of the large number of Scottish Protestant immigrant landlords, had allowed economic development; in fact, it led to a united Catholic-Protestant movement for independence. This United Irish movement and Irish Volunteers militia gained the Constitution of 1782, during the American War of Independence.

The Irish population had begun to grow rapidly in the last quarter of the Eighteenth Century.

Prime Minister William Pitt's policy was described by Sinn Fein's founder and Ireland's first President, Arthur Griffith.

On the 12th of May, 1785, Pitt's new proposals were introduced in the English Parliament. They provided, among other things, that Ireland should not trade with any country where its trading might clash with the interests of England's mightiest corporation—the East India Company ... and that the navigation laws which the British Parliament adopted should be accepted by Ireland.

Starving Irish peasants at the gates of a workhouse.

America and the Caribbean, agree that the Irish now were far worse off. In 1845, a British government commission headed by the economist Nassau Senior, confirmed that woolen, linen, poplin, furniture, and glass manufacture had disappeared; fishing had nearly disappeared for lack of capital for boats, storage, etc. Even water-powered grain mills had disappeared, in the country which had introduced them to Europe in 600 A.D. There were only 39 hospitals serving 8 million people.

The famous Duke of Wellington wrote in 1829 that "there never was a country in which poverty existed to the extent it exists in Ireland."

In 1824, a member of a previous British Commission had been asked in Parliament:

"Looking ahead to 15 years or more, what must this increase in population in Ireland, without any employment, end in?" Sounding like Sir David Attenborough today, he answered, "I don't know. I think it is terrible to reflect upon."

Once the famine was underway, the above-mentioned Nassau Senior wrote that he feared it would not kill more than a million people, which, he thought, would scarcely be enough to eliminate Irish unemployment.

But in 1842, 6 million pounds Sterling in rents were remitted out of Ireland to England, and a very large amount of real estate lending speculation in the City of London was based upon those rents.

Free Trade Without Money

Thus, when blight destroyed three-quarters of the potato crop of 1845, a sizeable majority of the Irish population owned no land, earned no wages, and paid as rent most or all of the proceeds of the sale of their grain crops. They had little or no money, or means of raising it; nearly two million did not even sell their

To enforce this, Pitt eventually provoked his own Irish armed revolt. His military repression of the Irish Uprising of 1798 disarmed the Irish Volunteers and introduced large numbers of British troops, to force the 1801 Act of Union which annulled the Irish Constitution. (During the same period, the same policy of the same Pitt and Shelburne also reduced and impoverished Scotland, which had begun to industrialize at the time of the American Revolution.)

In his political pamphlets, Arthur Griffith described in detail how Pitt, after 1801, destroyed Ireland's new manufactures, particularly linens, by dumping British goods there, and rapidly eliminated independent Irish shipping. Even worse, was the collapse in land use under Pitt's and Shelburne's policy. By the 1820s, 80% of all Ireland's land was owned by British and Scottish landlords, and 25% of all land was *completely unused* except for real estate speculation. Some 75% of what was used, was in grain or horse/cattle pasture, most of this for export by merchants under London's domination.

On the remainder, the Irish who worked for the British landlords were allowed to grow potatoes for themselves; on perhaps two acres of rented land for each large family.

All Nineteenth-Century accounts of those who saw both the Irish tenant farmers and African slaves in own produce, but turned it all over as rent in exchange for being allowed to grow potatoes on small strips of land.

Sir Robert Peel was British Prime Minister for the first half of 1846 after the destruction of the first potato crop. Immediately, a committee of Irish citizens (rather, subjects) headed by Henry Drummond made urgent proposals:

1. stop the export of corn and the distilling of grain into spirits;
2. remove duties on food imports;
3. public works concentrating on rail and harbor (fishing) infrastructure and drainage projects;
4. relief committees funded in part by a 10% tax on landlords (20-50% on absentees); and
5. in part by a 1.5 million pound, 10-year British loan on the security of Irish hardwood forests.

Prime Minister Peel responded by pushing for repeal of the British Corn Laws, to make import of Irish corn into Britain much easier.

Otherwise Peel's government bought, against a crop loss of 3.5 million pounds Sterling, a total of 100,000 pounds worth of American Indian corn, purchased through Baring Brothers' Bank. The reason for the tiny amount, was that it was to be locked up in military storehouses in Ireland, under control of Relief Commissioner Col. Henry Routh, and used "only as a leverage stock for purposes of preventing, through occasional sales from these stocks, an overfast rise in the market of foodstuffs."

Thirdly, Peel allowed formation of relief committees which could propose public works, but with no British government funds and solely voluntary (charitable) contributions from landlords in Ireland.

Treasury Head Sir Charles Trevelyan became effective dictator of the "relief" of Ireland, and already in June 1846 he was writing to Colonel Routh:

> The only way to prevent people from becoming habitually dependent on government, is to bring [relief] operations to a close. The uncertainty about the new crop [there were already signs of a second year of potato blight] only makes it more necessary.... These things should be stopped now, or you run the risk of paralyzing all private enterprise and having this country on you for an indefinite number of years.

Almost nothing of the tiny government "reserve stock" remained by then anyway. Baring's had one more ship on the way, but Trevelyan ordered that "the cargo of the *Sorciere* is not wanted; her owners must dispose of it as they think proper."

In September, when the Irish had begun to die of starvation, and there was plenty of evidence of the 100% failure of the 1846 second, annual potato crop, the *Times* of London added:

> Such are the thanks that a government gets for attempting to palliate great afflictions and satisfy corresponding demands by an inevitable but ruinous beneficence.... It is the old thing, the old malady, the national character, the national thoughtlessness, the national indolence.

Meanwhile, Peel's Tory government had been voted out for trying to repeal the Corn Laws—Great Britain's high tariffs on imported grain. Lord John Russell's Whig government replaced it and did get them repealed. During 1846, Ireland exported enough wheat, barley, oats, oatmeal, pigs, eggs, and butter to feed its entire population.

Many modern historians have raged at this export, which was heavily guarded by British troops against starving crowds. But few note that under British free trade policies, even more wheat was imported into Ireland that year than exported; however, at least half the entire Irish population was without any means to buy food; there was no government food support, and the rate of evictions was growing with the destitution.

Irish members of the British Parliament in London proposed the government buy stocks of grain otherwise to be exported, and sell it in the worst famine areas, especially in Connaught where starvation deaths were growing. The answer from Lord Russell directly was no: "Purchase by government of any food in ordinary use is forbidden in order to avoid competition with private traders."

Trevelyan and Colonel Routh agreed that

> there must be a distinction clearly kept between the ordinary distress of the people [!], and that resulting from the losses of the potato crop, which alone it may be our object to relieve.

Lord Russell's government added a Public Works program which was widespread but unfunded; local committees had to propose the works and sign a contract holding their members personally responsible to repay the British government 100% of the cost within two years, plus interest of 3% per annum! At first, the government sometimes added partial matching grants for local money raised, but these were very difficult to qualify for, and were completely discontinued in 1847. During all of 1846, with three million Irish unemployed and selling everything down to their family beds for food, a total of 5,000 pounds-Sterling was expended for piers, harbors, drainage, navigation and water power projects combined: In other words, none were carried out.

Russell and Trevelyan made a Public Works rule, which was later found as well in the Constitution of Jefferson Davis's Confederacy:

Any public works done shall not be of a nature to benefit any individuals in any greater degree than all of the rest of the community.

To the despair of the better-off Irish farmers who were trying to save their countrymen, this rule eliminated all projects for drainage of bogs—the only way to rapidly increase food production—on the grounds that this would preferentially benefit those living nearest the bog being drained.

This was the common argument against government infrastructure-building which was used against Abraham Lincoln's Illinois networks in the same years. As a result of this "rule," the Public Works during the Irish famine built only roads, which was the one kind of infrastructure which the country already had plenty of. The wages were supposedly set at subsistence levels, but as desperate people deluged the "Works," the wages were often paid weeks late, and many thousands starved to death. Meanwhile, in the Workhouses (called Poor Houses the next year after passage of the Irish Poor Law), several hundred thousand elderly, infirm, and young children crowded, dying more slowly of malnutrition and disease.

The Tavistock Grin

Lord John Russell evaluated the reports of the second consecutive complete failure of the potato crop as no reason to change policy. Lord Russell, the 6th Duke of Bedford, was known for his small stature and icy smile. By the winter of 1846-47, the Irish

people had begun to die of starvation in large numbers.

Lord Russell's Chancellor of the Exchequer, Sir Charles Wood, announced that there would be no more government importation of Indian corn or any other food—private enterprise would provide it. Public Works were to be limited to one year, and ended by Aug. 15, 1847, and their expense was "to fall entirely on persons possessed of property in the distressed district."

In Autumn 1846 crops failed in many European countries. French and German governments and bidders bought large amounts of grain from America and elsewhere, while the British government "sat it out." Food dealers in Ireland were now charging enormous prices, which Trevelyan welcomed in a letter to Colonel Routh:

The high prices will have a regulating influence, as nothing is more calculated to attract supplies, and especially from America.... Do not encourage the idea of prohibiting exports (from Ireland): perfect Free Trade is the right course. Nothing ought to be done for the West of Ireland which might send prices, already high, still higher for people who, unlike the inhabitants of the West Coast of Ireland, have to depend on their own exertions.

In December 1846 Whitehall ordered all Commissariat officers in Ireland to cease all food sales. Colonel Routh added in a memo:

Even if it were practicable at the moment to open our depots [he knew they were actually empty], it would be prejudicial to owners of grain, inasmuch as at present extraordinary prices can be realized.

If this seems an egregious government endorsement of price gouging, Trevelyan repeated it himself:

If dealers were to confine themselves to what in ordinary circumstances might be considered fair profits, the scarcity would be aggravated fearfully....

Trevelyan added that the government would also do

One of many mass evictions carried out by the British during the deepening Irish famine.

When Sir Charles Trevelyan, in February 1847, ordered the ending of all government "relief" spending, he added, "It is hard upon the poor people to be deprived of knowing that they are suffering from an affliction of God's Providence."

Only Lord Clarendon, the Viceroy for Ireland, remained the protesting voice: "What is to be done with these hordes? Improve them off the face of the earth, you will say, let them die. But there is a certain responsibility attaching to it."

'They Have Gone, Or Are Dead'

Typhus began to spread in March 1847. Trevelyan had his secretary notify all Poor Law Unions in July 1847:

> The Commissioners cannot but complain of finding the demands for rations from many districts continuously increasing, and sometimes largely, without even a word of explanation to account for it.

The entire cost of relief of the destitute and starving lay on the local "rates" paid by landlords. But, this threatened the London speculative bubble which Irish rents were sustaining. Lord Montcashel presented the following figures to the House of Lords: Of the annual rent collection in Ireland of 13 million pounds (a huge amount), the landlord class paid annually 10.5 million pounds-Sterling on "mortgages and borrowed money" to the City of London bankers and speculators in real estate. Montcashel was making clear that an increase in rates, now planned by the British government, would siphon money off from mortgage payments. Sure enough, in late summer 1847, the financial markets of London crashed, as the speculation in rents, wheat, corn, and foreign railway shares collapsed.

Landlords in Ireland now tried to evict all the tenants they could in order to reduce the number of local destitute, and therefore their rates (poor relief taxes). They began to get, not just evictions, but criminal judgments for non-payment of rent, throwing the fa-

nothing about the new problem—the disastrous fact that all seed potatoes had been eaten and there was nothing to plant in 1847: "The moment it came to be understood that the government would supply seed, the painful exertions of private initiative to preserve a stock of seed would be relaxed."

No seed would be provided, and, as it turned out, the 1847 potato harvest was to be blight-free, but only 20% of normal anyway for lack of seed and the death, exhaustion, or illness of farm families. The chance was not to be repeated: The 1848 crop again was destroyed by blight.

In January 1847, the British government smashed Circular #38, which the Irish Board of Public Works had issued, which would have allowed "family task work" under a sensible emergency proposal of some large farmers. It would have paid farm families wages to work their own land, and more wages for also working on drainage projects. "It is quite impossible," wrote Trevelyan, "for my lords to give their sanction to parties being paid by public funds for the cultivation of their own land." The government also defeated a proposal of Lord George Bentinck in Parliament, for a railroad building act in Ireland funded by the British Treasury.

That same month, Colonel Routh reported on Ireland's poorest county, Skibereen, that 50,000 pounds rent had been paid in 1846; there were only twelve landowners, all British lords and knights.

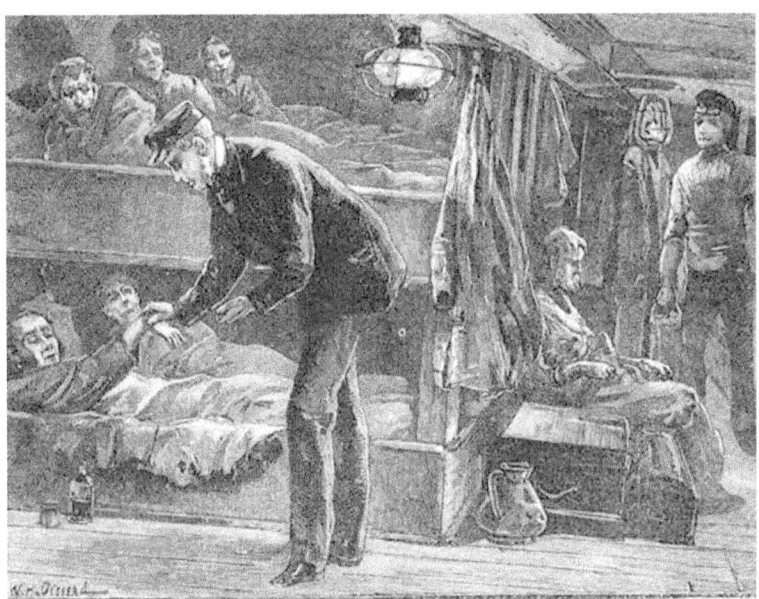

A scene from a ship carrying some of the millions of Irish who fled to North America during the depths of the famine.

thers of families into jail. This—as the landlords intended—finally set off the migration across the Atlantic which became a flood of starving, dying typhus-carriers into Canada and then New England in 1848-9.

Incredibly, large exports of foodstuffs from Ireland continued right through 1848 and 1849, which were the years in which the Irish population fell rapidly from 8.2 million to six million through death and emigration (and 40% of the emigrants died in crossing the Atlantic alone). In November 1848, exports of food from the County of Cork in a single day, were 147 bales of bacon, 255 barrels of pork, 5 casks of hams, 3,000 sacks and barrels of oats, 300 bags of flour, 300 head of cattle, 239 sheep, 542 boxes of eggs, 9,300 firkins [about one-fourth of a barrel] of butter, and 150 casks of miscellaneous foodstuffs.

But an inspector of the Public Works in Cork in the same month wrote about the public "workfare" rolls: "The lists are useless. No one answers their name. They have gone, or are dead."

1848 was the year in which "revolutions" and insurrections took place against those European governments targetted by the British, particularly France. Foreign Minister Lord Palmerston personally manipulated and directed the "Young Europe" agents who fomented these insurrections. A very small and pathetic such "uprising" was apparently attempted that year by the "Young Ireland" movement; but in fact, Lord Russell had written to Palmerston three months earlier, acknowledging that this "Young Ireland" was controlled by Palmerston. "I am not yet ready to adopt, like Mr. Pitt, 'ripening measures' to force on a rebellion," wrote Russell in December 1847. Thus he was admitting, at the same time, that the Irish Uprising of 1798 had been sponsored and controlled by then-Prime Minister William Pitt, in order to force upon Ireland the ruinous Act of Union in place of the Irish Constitution of 1782.

Palmerston still found time to evict nine shiploads full of his Irish tenants to Canada, 2,000 persons in all. As the ships arrived in New Brunswick, they raised storms of protest—on board children, elderly, and destitute were starving, many of them completely naked: "They had to be clothed by charity before they could, with decency, leave the ship." The "Common Council of the City of St. John deeply regret that one of Her Majesty's ministers, the Rt. Hon. Lord Palmerston ... should have exposed such a numerous and distressed portion of his tenantry to the severity and privations of a New Brunswick winter ... unprovided with the common means of support, with broken-down constitutions and almost in a state of nudity."

Ireland has never recovered from Britain's Nineteenth-Century episode in "reducing carrying capacity." In Lyndon LaRouche's terms, from 1800 1850 British colonial policy succeeded in reducing the "potential population density" of Ireland—which is relative to its use of energy, agricultural, and industrial technology—to far below the *actual* Irish population of eight million in 1800. And so 2.5 million of them disappeared: two million dead of starvation and disease; 500,000 barely alive in America.

Ireland's scant industrial and agricultural progress in the Twentieth Century is due entirely to the national institutions built by the Sinn Fein movement of 1902-1924, which explicitly opposed British free-trade dogma. But once again in the financial crash of 2007-08, Ireland was initially thrown backwards farther and faster than any other European country, because of the debt bubbles which London-centered banks had blown on Irish soil. Ireland's potential relative population density was again thrust down—now below five million in the Republic—by British policy.

British Colonials Starved to Death 60 million-plus Indians, But, Why?

by Ramtanu Maitra

The chronic want of food and water, the lack of sanitation and medical help, the neglect of means of communication, the poverty of educational provision, the all-pervading spirit of depression that I have myself seen to prevail in our villages after over a hundred years of British rule make me despair of its beneficence.
— Rabindranath Tagore

If the history of British rule in India were to be condensed to a single fact, it is this: there was no increase in India's per-capita income from 1757 to 1947.[1]

Churchill, explaining why he defended the stockpiling of food within Britain, while millions died of starvation in Bengal, told his private secretary that "the Hindus were a foul race, protected by their mere pullulation from the doom that is their due."[2]

June 27—During its 190 years of looting and pillaging, the Indian Subcontinent as a whole underwent at least two dozen major famines, which collectively killed millions of Indians throughout the length and breadth of the land. How many millions succumbed to the famines cannot be fully ascertained. However, colonial rulers' official numbers indicate it could be 60 million deaths. In reality, it could be significantly higher.

British colonial analysts cited droughts as the cause of fallen agricultural production that led to these famines, but that is a lie. British rulers, fighting wars in Europe and elsewhere, and colonizing parts of Africa, were exporting grains from India to keep up their colonial conquests—while famines were raging. People in the famine-affected areas, resembling skeletons covered by skin only, were wandering around, huddling in corners and dying by the millions. The Satanic nature of these British rulers cannot be overstated.

A Systematic Depopulation Policy

Although no accurate census figure is available, in the year 1750 India's population was close to 155 million. At the time British colonial rule ended in 1947, undivided India's population reached close to 390 million. In other words, during these 190 years of colonial looting and organized famines, India's population rose by 240 million. Since 1947, during the next 68-year period, Indian Subcontinent's population, including those of India, Paki-

The "Butcher of Bombay," the British East India Company's Baron Robert Clive, in a painting by Nathaniel Dance.

1. Davis, Mike. *Late Victorian Holocausts: El Nino Famines and the Making of the Third World*, London, Verso Books, 2001.
2. Madhusree Mukerjee, *Churchill's Secret War: The British Empire and the Ravaging of India during World War II*, New York: Basic Books.

20   Are You a Dupe of Satan?

EIR   July 3, 2015

stan, and Bangladesh, has grown to close to 1.6 billion. Thus, despite poverty and economic depravity in the post-independent Indian Subcontininent, during those 68 years population has grown by almost 1.2 billion.

Records show that during the post-independence period, the Subcontininent has undergone drought conditions in parts of the land from time to time, but there was no famine, although thousands still die in the Subcontininent annually due to the lack of adequate amount of food, a poor food distribution system, and lack of sufficient nourishment. It is also to be noted that before the British colonials' jackboots got firmly planted in India, famines had occurred but with much less frequency—maybe once in a century.

There was indeed no reason for these famines to occur They occurred only because The Empire engineered them, intending to strengthen the Empire by ruthless looting and adoption of an unstated policy to depopulate India. This, they believed would bring down the Empire's cost of sustaining India.

Take, for instance, the case of Bengal, which is in the eastern part of the Subcontininent where the British East India Company (HEIC, Honorable East India Company, according to Elizabeth I's charter) had first planted its jackboots in 1757. The rapacious looters, under the leadership of Robert Clive—a degenerate and opium addict, who blew his brains out in 1774 in the London Berkley Square residence he had procured with the benefits of his looting—got control of what is now West Bengal, Bangladesh, Bihar, and Odisha (earlier, Orissa), in 1765. At the time, historical records indicate India represented close to 25% of the world's GDP, second only to China, while Britain had a paltry 2%. Bengal was the richest of the Indian provinces.

Following his securing control of Bengal by ousting the Nawab in a devious battle at Plassey (Palashi), Clive placed a puppet on the throne, paid him off, and negotiated an agreement with him for the HEIC to become the sole tax collector, while leaving the nominal responsibility for government to his puppet. That arrangement lasted for a century, as more and more Indian states were bankrupted to facilitate future famines. The tax money went into British coffers, while millions were starved to death in Bengal and Bihar.

Clive, who was made a Fellow of the Royal Society in 1768 and whose statue stands near the British Empire's evil center, Whitehall, near the Cabinet War Room, had this to say in his defense when the British Parliament, playing "fair," accused him of looting and other abuses in India:

> Consider the situation which the Victory of Plassey had placed on me. A great Prince was dependent upon my pleasure; an opulent city lay at my mercy; its richest bankers bid against each other for my smiles; I walked through vaults which were thrown open to me alone, piled on either hand with gold and jewels! By God, Mr. Chairman, at this moment I stand astonished at my own moderation.

However, Clive was not the only murderous British colonial ruler. The British Empire had sent one butcher after another to India, all of whom engineered looting and its consequent depopulation.

By 1770, when the first great famine occurred in Bengal, the province had been looted to the core. What followed was sheer horror. Here is how John Fiske in his *American Philosopher in the Unseen World* depicted the Bengal famine:

> All through the stifling summer of 1770 the people went on dying. The husbandmen sold their cattle; they sold their implements of agriculture; they devoured their seed-grain; they sold their sons and daughters, till at length no buyer of children could be found; they ate the leaves of trees and the grass of the field.... The streets were blocked up with promiscuous heaps of the dying and dead. Interment could not do its work quick enough; even the dogs and jackals, the public scavengers of the East, became unable to accomplish their revolting work, and the multitude of mangled and festering corpses at length threatened the existence of the citizens....[3]

Was there any reason for the famine to occur? Not if the British had not wanted it. Bengal, then, as now, harvested three crops a year. It is located in the delta of the Gangetic plain where water is more than plentiful. Even if drought occurs, it does not destroy all three crops. Moreover, as was prevalent during the Moghul days, and in earlier time, the surplus grain was stored to tide the population over if there were one or two bad crops.

---

3. Davis, op. cit.

The Great Famine of 1887-78 was depicted thus in the Illustrated London News *in 1877, with the caption "The famine in India—natives waiting for relief in Bangalore."*

But the looting of grains carried out by Clive, and his gang of bandits and killers, drained grain from Bengal and resulted in 10 million deaths in the great famine, eliminating *one-third* of Bengal's population.

It should be noted that Britain's much-touted industrial revolution began in 1770, the very same year people were dying all over Bengal. The Boston Tea Party that triggered the American Revolution had taken place in 1773. The Boston Tea Party made the Empire realize that its days in America were numbered, and led Britain to concentrate even more on organizing the looting of India.

Why Famines Became So Prevalent During the British Raj Days

The prime reason why these devastating famines took place at a regular intervals, and were allowed to continue for years, was the British Empire's policy of depopulating its colonies. If these famines had not oc-

curred, India's population would have reached a billion people long before the Twentieth Century arrived. That, the British Empire saw as a disaster.

To begin with, a larger Indian population would mean larger consumption by the locals, and deprive the British Raj to a greater amount of loot. The logical way to deal with the problem was to develop India's agricultural infrastructure. But that would not only force Britain to spend more money to run its colonial and bestial empire; it would also develop a healthy population which could rise up to get rid of the abomination called the British Raj. These massive famines also succeeded in weakening the social structure and backbone of the Indians, making rebellions against the colonial forces less likely.

In order to perpetuate famines, and thus depopulate the "heathen" and "dark" Indians, the British imperialists launched a systematic propaganda campaign. They propped up the fraudster Parson Thomas Malthus and promoted his non-scientific gobbledygook, "The Essay on Population." There he claimed:

This natural inequality of the two powers of population and of production in the earth, and that great law of our nature which must constantly keep their effects equal, form the great difficulty that to me appears insurmountable in the way to the perfectibility of society. All other arguments are of slight and subordinate consideration in comparison of this. I see no way by which man can escape from the weight of this law which pervades all animated nature.

Although Malthus was ordained in the Anglican Church, British Empire made him a paid "economist" of the British East India Company, which, with the charter from Queen Elizabeth I under its belt, monopolized trade in Asia, colonizing vast tracts of the continent using its well-armed militia fighting under the English flag of St. George.

Malthus was picked up at the Haileybury and Imperial Service College, which was also the recruiting ground of some of the worst colonial criminals. This college was where the makers of British Empire's murderous policies in India were trained. Some prominent alumni of Haileybury include Sir John Lawrence (Viceroy of India from 1864-68) and Sir Richard Temple (Lt. Governor of Bengal and later, Governor of Bombay presidency).

While Parson Malthus was putting forward his sinister "scientific theory" to justify depopulation as a natural and necessary process, The British Empire collected a whole bunch of other "economists" who wrote about the necessity of free trade. Free trade played a major role in pushing through the Empire's genocidal depopulation of India, through the British Raj's efforts. In fact, free trade is the other side of the Malthus' population-control coin.

By the time the great famine of 1876 arrived, Britain had already built some railroads in India. The railroads, which were touted as institutional safeguards against famines, were instead used by merchants to ship grain inventories from outlying drought-stricken districts to central depots for hoarding. In addition, free traders' opposition to price control ushered in a frenzy of grain speculation. As a result, capital was raised to import grains from drought-stricken areas, and further the calamity. The rise of price of grain was spectacularly rapid, and grain was taken from where it was most needed, to be stored in warehouses until the prices rose even higher.

The British Raj knew or should have known. Even if the British rulers did not openly encourage this process, they were fully aware of it, and they were perfectly comfortable in promoting free trade at the expense of millions of lives. This is how Mike Davis described what happened:

The rise [of prices] was so extraordinary, and the available supply, as compared with well-known requirements, so scanty that merchants and dealers, hopeful of enormous future gains, appeared determined to hold their stocks for some indefinite time and not to part with the article which was becoming of such unwonted value. It was apparent to the Government that facilities for moving grain by the rail were rapidly raising prices everywhere, and that the activity of apparent importation and railway transit, did not indicate any addition to the food stocks of the Presidency....retail trade up-country was almost at a standstill. Either prices were asked which were

beyond the means of the multitude to pay, or shops remained entirely closed.

At the time, Lord Lytton, a favorite poet of Queen Victoria who is known as a "butcher" to many Indians, was the Viceroy. He wholeheartedly opposed all efforts to stockpile grain to feed the famine-stricken population because that would interfere with market forces. In the autumn of 1876, while the monsoon crop was withering in the fields of southern India, Lytton was absorbed in organizing the immense Imperial Assemblage in Delhi to proclaim Victoria Empress of India.

How did Lytton justify this? He was an avowed admirer and follower of Adam Smith. Author Mike Davis writes that Smith

a century earlier in *The Wealth of Nations* had asserted (vis-à-vis the terrible Bengal drought-famine of 1770) that famine has never arisen from any other cause but the violence of government attempting, by improper means, to remedy the inconvenience of dearth, Lytton was implementing what Smith had taught him and other believers of free trade. Smith's injunction against state attempts to regulate the price of grain during the 1770 famine had been taught for years in the East India Company's famous college at Haileybury.[4]

Lytton issued strict orders that "there is to be no interference of any kind on the part of Government with the object of reducing the price of food," and "in his letters home to the India Office and to politicians of both parties, he denounced 'humanitarian hysterics'." By official diktat, India, like Ireland before it, had become a Utilitarian laboratory where millions of lives were gambled, pursuant to dogmatic faith in omnipotent markets overcoming the "inconvenience of dearth."[5]

The Great Famines
Depicting the two dozen famines that killed more than 60 million Indians would require a lot of space, so I limit myself here to those that killed more than one million:

The Bengal Famine of 1770: This catastrophic

---

4. Ibid.
5. Ibid.

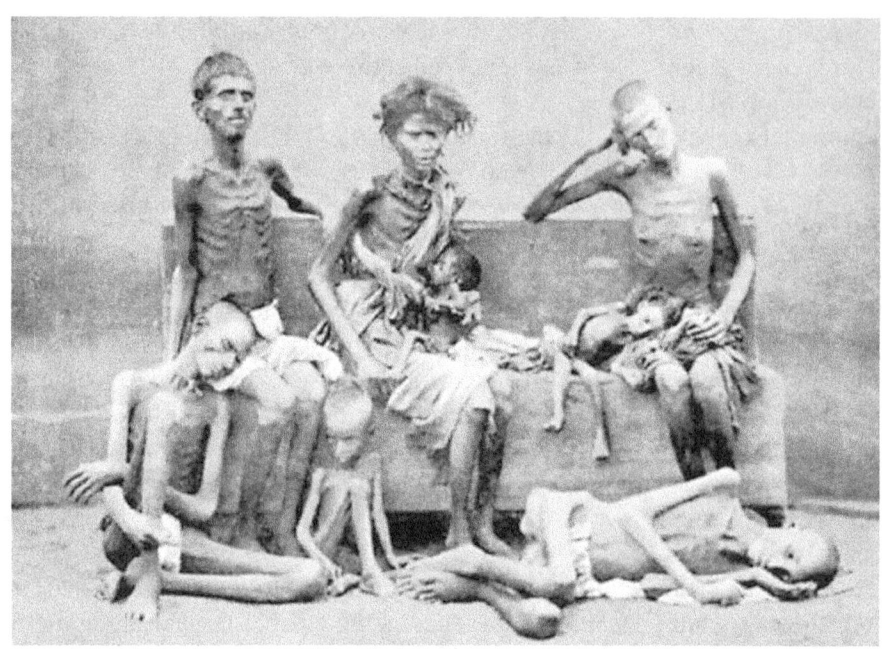
Victims of the "modern" Indian famine induced by the Winston Churchill, the Bengali Famine of 1943.

famine occurred between 1769 and 1773, and affected the lower Gangetic plain of India. The territory, then ruled by the British East India Company, included modern West Bengal, Bangladesh, and parts of Assam, Orissa, Bihar, and Jharkhand. The famine is supposed to have caused the deaths of an estimated 10 million people, approximately one-third of the population at the time.

The Chalisa Famine of 1783-84: The Chalisa famine affected many parts of North India, especially the Delhi territories, present-day Uttar Pradesh, Eastern Punjab, Rajputana (now named, Rajasthan), and Kashmir, then all ruled by different Indian rulers. The Chalisa was preceded by a famine in the previous year, 1782-83, in South India, including Madras City (now named Chennai) and surrounding areas (under British East India Company rule), and in the extended Kingdom of Mysore. Together, these two famines had taken at least 11 million lives, reports indicate.

The Doji Bara Famine (or Skull Famine) of 1791-92: This famine caused widespread mortality in Hyderabad, Southern Maratha Kingdom, Deccan, Gujarat, and Marwar (also called Jodhpur region in Rajasthan). The British policy of diverting food to Europe, of pricing the remaining grain out of reach of native Indians, and adopting agriculture policy that destroyed food production, was responsible for this one. The British

had surplus supplies of grain, which was not distributed to the very people that had grown it. As a result, about 11 million died between 1789-92 of starvation and accompanying epidemics that followed.

The Upper Doab Famine of 1860-61: The 1860-61 famine occurred in the British-controlled Ganga-Yamuna Doab (two waters, or two rivers) area engulfing large parts of Rohilkhand and Ayodhya, and the Delhi and Hissar divisions of the then-Punjab. Eastern part of the princely state of Rajputana. According to "official" British reports, about two million people were killed by this famine.

The Orissa Famine of 1866: Although it affected Orissa the most, this famine affected India's east coast along the Bay of Bengal stretching down south to Madras, covering a vast area. One million died, according to the British "official" version.

The Rajputana famine of 1869: The Rajputana famine of 1869 affected an area of close to 300,000 square miles which belonged mostly to the princely states and the British territory of Ajmer. This famine, according to "official" British claim, killed 1.5 million.

The Great Famine of 1876-78: This famine killed untold numbers of Indians in the southern part and raged for about four years. It affected Madras, Mysore, Hyderabad and Bombay (now called, Mumbai). The famine also subsequently visited Central Province (now called, Madhya Pradesh) and parts of undivided Punjab. The death toll from this famine was in the range of 5.5 million people. Some other figures indicate the number of deaths could be as high as 11 million.

Indian famine of 1896-97 and 1899-1900: This one affected Madras, Bombay, Deccan, Bengal, United Provinces (now called, Uttar Pradesh), Central Provinces, Northern and eastern Rajputana, parts of Central India, and Hyderabad: six million reportedly died in British territory during these two famines. The number of deaths occurred in the princely states is not known.

The Bengal Famine of 1943-44: This Churchill-

Distribution of famine relief in the Madras area, from the Illustrated London News, *May 26, 1877.*

orchestrated famine in Bengal in 1943-1944 killed an estimated 3.5 to 5 million people.

Relief Camps, or Concentration camps

There were several policy-arrows which Adolf Hitler might have borrowed from the British quiver to kill millions, but one that he borrowed for certain in setting up his death camps, was how the British ran the camps to provide "relief" to the starving millions. Anyone who entered these relief camps, did not exit alive.

Take the actions of Viceroy Lytton's deputy, Richard Temple, another Haileybury product imbued with the doctrine of depopulation as the necessary means to keep the Empire strong and vigorous. Temple was under orders from Lytton to make sure there was no "unnecessary" expenditure on relief works.

According to some analysts, Temple's camps were not very different from Nazi concentration camps. People already half-dead from starvation had to walk hundreds of miles to reach these relief camps. Additionally, he instituted a food ration for starving people working in the camps, which was less than that was given to the inmates of Nazi concentration camps.

The British refused to provide adequate relief for famine victims on the grounds that this would encourage indolence. Sir Richard Temple, who was selected to organize famine relief efforts in 1877, set the food allotment for starving Indians at 16 ounces of rice per day—less than the diet for inmates at the Buchenwald concentration camp for the Jews in Hitler's Germany. British disinclination to respond with urgency and vigor to food deficits resulted in a succession of about two dozen appalling famines during the British occupation of India. These swept away tens of millions of people. The frequency of famine showed a disconcerting increase in the nineteenth century.[6]

It was deliberate then, and it's deliberate now.

6. Bhatia, B.M., *Famines in India, A Study in Some Aspects of the Economic History of India, 1860-1945*, Asia Publishing House, Bombay, 1963.

Nino Galloni on the Papal Encyclical on the Environment

Antonino Galloni is an Italian economist who worked as director general of the Budget and Labor Ministries in the early 1990s. He has taught in the Universities of Naples, Rome (LUISS), Milan, and Modena. Currently, he is major auditor at the National Institute of National and Social Services (INPS), which manages the national pension fund. He has published many books and articles.

The following article was published in Il Domani d'Italia, *a progressive Catholic publication (http://ildomaniditalia.eu/article/la-lezione-dellenciclica-non-pu%C3%B2-consistere-nel-richiamo-buoni-propositi-bisogna-cambiare), and republished on scenarieconomici.it, a website run by anti-euro economists. A subhead has been added.*

The Encyclical issued by Pope Francis on the environment merits in-depth examination. The Pope highlights the schizophrenia of our systems, which are capable of producing more than what we need, while billions of human beings continue to live in abject poverty. We will talk more about this later, but here is the problem: our models are all based on ephemerals, on waste and useless (or even harmful) consumption, agreed: but what is the alternative model?

Well, let us eliminate the useless product and redistribute the excess (the parable of the rich man and Lazarus); behold the degrowth model! It calls itself happy, but happy it is not: the degrowth model, in fact, to be sustainable and not un-

realistic, demands that demographic decline be greater than the decline in production. Thus, you cannot endorse economic degrowth without endorsing depopulation.

The solution proposed by the Encyclical is to distribute resources equitably. Therefore, to make the analytical logic of degrowth (whose criticism of the system may be shared, and I believe, is shared by the Pope) compatible with a rejection of demographic decline, one must propose a model in which those who have more, deprive themselves of a portion of it, so that everyone gets enough.

The world has never worked that way: today, as was the case before the democracies of the Twentieth Century, scarcity,—genuine in the past, artificial today,—means an unfair distribution of resources and income because only the rich can make the investments necessary for the survival of the entire society. By contrast, with the coming into being of democratic regimes, which were then abandoned about thirty years ago, growth across the board was promoted, which improved the well-being of the lower classes, promoted the middle class and satisfied the affluent.

The same applies to the prospects of strategic resources, first of all water, in the Encyclical. It fails to call for projects to develop our current desalination capacities, to collect water from glacial melt, or by altering the flow of the Nile River (to name only a few examples). These would only utilize mankind's current techno-

Schiller Institute

Prof. Nino Galloni, addressing the 30th Anniversary Conference of the Schiller Institute in Germany, October 18-19, 2014.

logical capacities, but the Encyclical only calls on us to accept a more equitable distribution of resources.

Whereas technological progress has not solved the defense of biodiversity dilemma (paragraph 33), perhaps the mention of the Congo Basin (39) can be used to sharpen our reasoning. The Congolese population, despite wars, genocide, disease, and misery, has increased. Therefore what caused the elimination of almost all the local fauna, was poverty multiplied by increasing numbers. Misery, accompanied by demographic growth, has catastrophic effects on the environment and on biodiversity, which can only be prevented by technological progress, and increasing energy flux intensity. A small community can survive on a given territory by chopping wood and hunting animals, provided that their low numbers do not jeopardize the balance.

Change the Model

As the population grows, the model must change. Energy flux must be intensified, production technologies must change. There is no need to reduce individual consumption of resources if the population is growing; the amount of resources consumed per unit of product needs to be reduced: exactly what technology, in other words, human intelligence, is able to guarantee.

Thus, concerning Chapter II of the Encyclical, it is sufficient neither to stress that man has no right to destroy nature, nor that he should be responsible (both sacrosanct, of course),—but it is also necessary to accept the idea that man can transform nature by intervening in it; if that were not so, it would be impossible,—except marginally,—to reduce our use of resources while maintaining demographic growth.

The Encyclical seems to fear technology and the transformation (reasonable, partial, etc.) of nature, to the point of confirming, in Chapter III, at the end of paragraph 106, the thesis of the Justitia et Pax Commission according to which "there is no unlimited energy." On the contrary, new technologies can already supply energy at zero cost, but the problem is that this cannot be done by the large multinationals. Why produce without profit? And so, the big lacuna in the Encyclical is the absence of a capitalist model based on state enterprises, i.e., a non-capitalistic model.

Also, when the Encyclical denies anthropocentrism, I do not understand how this coheres with the centrality of man correctly cited from *Gaudium et Spes* [of the Second Vatican Council]. See paragraph 127.

The last three chapters are exhortations, sound principles, a reference to the common good, to a feeling of inter-generational solidarity as well as solidarity with immigrants. They are all points which we can agree on, and are important to stress; but their weakness stems from the type of economic model that began to marginalize the real economy about 30 years ago, to clear the way for increasingly devastating, if not delusionary, forms of financialization of the economy.

And so, since the Encyclical shares this critique, and given the fact that it has gone beyond a merely pastoral role (a good thing, or rather, an excellent thing, which reflects the gravity of the moral and social situation in which we find ourselves), why not complete the work by not just approving desirable behaviors, but also by pushing towards new models?

The critical issue of degrowth is intriguing, but not compatible with our theology when it comes to demographic trends; an inspired view of technological progress, which minimizes polluting agents and non-renewable resources per unit of product (rather than merely calling for reduction of consumption and equitable distribution), is compatible.

—*Nino Galloni*

Zepp-LaRouche, Yiwu Forum Focus on Promise of Silk Road

by William Jones

June 26—Speaking on June 19 at the Silk Road Economic Belt Cities International Forum in Yiwu, China, Helga Zepp-LaRouche, president of the Schiller Institute, warned of the dangers facing the world of possible financial blowout and global war, and underlined the importance of the Silk Road Economic Belt, proposed by Chinese President Xi Jinping, as the way out of the crisis.

The June 18-19 forum had been organized by the Chongyang Institute of Financial Studies at Renmin University, huanqiu.com—a division of Global Times newspaper, and the Yiwu City Peoples Government. While the conference focused on Yiwu, a growing city south of Shanghai, as a hub at the end of the new train corridor between Asia and Europe, the conference organizers had brought together an impressive group of people internationally to underline the importance of this project for the world as a whole.

EIRNS

Helga Zepp-LaRouche, third from the right, with her fellow panelists at the Silk Road Economic Belt Cities International Forum in Yiwu, China, June 19, 2015.

Pointing to the dangers stemming from a possible Greek default, Zepp-LaRouche told the several hundred people gathered there:

> A chaotic collapse can be prevented only if the EU and European nations agree to convene a European debt conference in the tradition of the 1953 Debt Conference for Germany, which laid the basis for the German miracle of the postwar period.

She pointed to the need for a return to the policy of industrial banking of German bankers Hermann Abs and Alfred Herrhausen, who followed in the tradition of the American System of Economy of Alexander Hamilton.

She noted the importance of German industrial capabilities, especially the innovative small and middle-sized firms, the Mittelstand, in bringing the world out of the financial crisis. Germany is also crucial diplomatically. If Germany were to reject the push to war emanating from the policy of the United States and NATO, there would be no war. Leading politicians in Germany, she said, realize that the sanctions are aimed against Germany as well as Russia, with German exports to Russia falling by 28% in the first quarter of this year.

> If Germany would now end the sanctions by admitting that the reason for the crisis is not Russia but the EU itself in its pushing the EU Association Agreement on Ukraine, then this crisis could be overcome.

She referred to the comments of Gottfried Leibniz in one of his major writings on China, *Novissima Sinica*, that if Europe and China, those two great cultures at opposite sides of Eurasia, would come together in cooperation, all the countries in the world would benefit.

Her speech, which stood out starkly from the other presentations from representatives of other European countries who were to discuss their role in the Silk Road Economic Belt, created a flurry of interest, not least of all in the new report which, as she noted in her speech, had been put out by the Schiller Institute and *EIR*, entitled "The New Silk Road Becomes the World Land-bridge".

EIRNS

EIR's Washington Bureau Chief William Jones intervenes in the Silk Road Forum.

In introducing Zepp-LaRouche, the moderator of the panel noted that in Europe she is widely considered the initiator of the New Silk Road concept.

After the forum, many people came up to talk, and to view the report. Her speech also garnered widespread attention by the media, with one article circulating on sina.com, an equivalent to Yahoo or Google in the U.S., translating and quoting almost all of her ten-minute speech.

Many other websites and papers borrowed extensively from the sina.com article in their comments in the following days. Others noted her response in the Q&A session, where she succinctly noted the need for high-speed rail—as opposed to sea transport—since in a high-tech, high-value economy, speed of transport of goods becomes a premium.

High-Level Presence Draws Attention

While Yiwu is only one of a number of cities in China holding conferences on the Silk Road Economic Belt in an effort to profile their importance in the project, Yiwu's geographical location, less than one hundred miles from Ningbo, the nearest port, and at the terminal of the European rail line, served to spark more than local interest. Also, since the organizers had assembled a high-level presence at the conference—including two former prime ministers, and a former foreign minister, as well as a representative from the

Foreign Affairs Committee of the National Peoples Congress, and numerous ambassadors to the Peoples Republic of China—there was considerable nationwide media attention focused on this conference. A short interview with *EIR*'s Washington correspondent Bill Jones, given to the local Yiwu TV, was also aired nationally by CCTV in its coverage of the forum.

While Yiwu is not a major industrial center, it has transformed itself into a major commodities port, with goods coming in from all of Southeast Asia through the port of Ningbo for shipment and transfer through Yiwu to Central Asia and Europe, over the new rail lines. So too, goods from Europe are brought by rail to the Yiwu land port before shipment by sea to other parts of the Asia-Pacific.

The two-day event also featured numerous panels on various aspects of the Silk Road project. At a panel on "The Silk Road: New Starting Point", *EIR*'s Bill Jones was quizzed on the attitude of the United States to this project. Jones noted the need for bringing the United States on board the project for its own sake. When one Chinese scholar expressed skepticism that the United States would ever be willing to cooperate in this project by China, Jones described the devastation to the U.S.

economy as a result of the failed economic policies of the Bush and Obama Administrations, starkly underlined by the absolute failure to respond effectively to the tremendous drought in California. "Our infrastructure is in a shambles," Jones said, "and people understand that only with the orientation toward massive infrastructural investment as expressed by the Silk Road project can the United States survive," he said. "And even now, many states of the Union are coming to China to encourage China to invest in their infrastructure as well."

It was clear that the organizers of the conference considered the presence of the Schiller Institute very prestigious for their event. While the ex-ministers and the ambassadors might have helped to bring added media attention to the conference, the intellectual rigor exhibited by Helga Zepp-LaRouche in her speech, really placed her in a category of her own. This was evident to all who heard her remarks, bringing a clear—and stark—note of reality to an event which otherwise might have been simply a worthwhile rally for a praiseworthy project. Her short speech and the media coverage of it, as well as the separate interviews she gave during the conference, will reverberate widely in China and beyond.

Zepp-LaRouche China Speech: Silk Road Can Lead World out of Collapse and War

Speech of Helga Zepp-LaRouche at Silk Road Economic Belt Cities International Forum, Yiwu, China, June 19, 2015.

The New Silk Road is not only an extremely important economic initiative. Because it is a win-win perspective, it also addresses the two biggest dangers in the world today: the danger of a financial blowout of the trans-Atlantic sector and the danger of global war. I have to address the fact that if the hardline of the Troika insists that Greece should pay the debt, a debt of 360 billion euros which is completely unpayable, this will blow out the derivatives of the European and American banking system.

Two days ago, the Debt Truth Commission of the Greek Parliament found the Greek debt to be illegitimate, odious, and unpayable. Now, the debt blowout can be prevented if there is a European debt conference in the tradition of the 1953 Debt Conference for Germany, which was the precondition for the economic miracle of Germany to occur. If there is a credit policy adopted in the tradition of the Kreditanstalt für Wiederaufbau [Credit Institution for Reconstruction], given the importance of its role in the reconstruction of Germany in the postwar period, this would mean going back to industrial banking in the tradition of Hermann Abs or Alfred Herrhausen, who were in the tradition of Alexander Hamilton, the founder of the American System of Economy in the United States.

The German economy is key to the situation, because there are many people in Germany—including retired members of the military, industrialists, and two former Chancellors, Helmut Schmidt and Gerhard Schröder, and Foreign Minister Frank-Walter Steinmeier—who realize that the G7 has been turned into a geopolitical tool of confrontation against Russia. And they also realize, many of them, that Germany is as much a target of this geopolitical confrontation as Russia.

For German industry is collapsing right now, losing 28% of its exports to Russia in the first quarter of this year. But in spite of the erosion of the German economy due to the nuclear "exit" three or four years ago, Germany still remains the economic powerhouse of Europe. And if Germany would now end the sanctions by admitting that the reason for the crisis is not Russia, but the EU itself, by pushing the EU Association Agreement, then this crisis could be overcome.

Now with the upcoming summit of the European Fund for Strategic Investment on the 29th of June which China's Premier of the State Council Li Keqiang will attend, this could become a venue to co-finance the extension of the New Silk Road to Southern Europe, and in that way address this problem.

Already in 2012, the Schiller Institute produced a comprehensive program for the development of the Mediterranean Basin Great Infrastructure Projects, which would extend the New Silk Road to all of south-

EIRNS

Helga Zepp-LaRouche being interviewed after her intervention at the Yiwu Silk Road Forum.

ern Europe. It was based essentially on the proposal which the EU had already agreed upon at its conference in Crete in 1994: that ten transportation corridors be built. But they were never created because of the austerity policy of the EU.

This was also the subject at the big conferences in Bucharest and Belgrade which Li Keqiang attended in 2013 and 2014. If this program were to be implemented, then Greece would become the bridge between Europe and the BRICS, and build on the ancient collaboration of Greece and China, at a time when Greece was the transport hub for the ancient Silk Road, and would build on the old ties of the two great cultures of Greece and China.

50%-Plus of Expenditure on Infrastructure

Now the quality and density of infrastructure is a precondition for the productivity of the economy. A modern economy should invest at least 50% of its total expenditure in infrastructure. We are not talking about connections between point

EIRNS

Zepp-LaRouche (right) chats with a fellow panelist.

A and point B, but we are talking about corridors which will consist of high-speed rail, waterways, highways, energy production and distribution, and communications, because this is what governs the conditions for optimally locating industrial production and agriculture.

The purpose of these corridors is to increase the productivity of the population. The connection between the many ends of the New Silk Road in Yiwu, but also in Lianyungang and other places, to Duisburg, is one good example to show that the higher the development and productivity of an economy, the more important the speed and efficiency of transport. Because then the finished and semi-finished goods work together like a complex machine where each part functions as a part of a harmonious whole. The density of infrastructure in the Ruhr and Baden-WÜrttemberg and in Rhein-Main should become the model for the Balkans and southern Italy and the Aegean Peninsula.

To get the world out of the geostrategic confrontation with Xi Jinping's "win-win" Silk Road policy, the integration of the German economy is absolutely crucial. For Germany presently ranks as number four in the number of registered patents in the world; and this with a population of only 80 million people. And the high ratio of the so-called Mittelstand, mid-level German industries, which are largely innovation-based firms using

essential machine tools and machine-tool designs, is crucial for bringing the world out of its present crisis.

The Schiller Institute has produced a study of 370 pages entitled "The New Silk Road Becomes the World Land-Bridge," which is essentially an outline for the next decade of how to overcome the underdevelopment of large areas of the world. These are the corridors which will connect the world from the southern tip of Chile, all the way through the Americas to the Bering Strait, and then to the tip of South Africa.

This would mean cooperation in the areas of high energy-flux density industries like biophysics and space exploration. This project presents limitless possibilities for a "win-win" cooperation of the whole world.

Gottfried Leibniz in *Novissima Sinica* wrote more than 300 years ago:

> The two most advanced cultures on the planet are located at opposite poles of the Eurasian continent, and that if these two poles join hands, then every region in between can be uplifted.

Now this vision today is true for the whole world. Together we can create a new era in human history where the human species is able to overcome geopolitics forever, and develop its true identity as the only creative species so far known in the universe.

Yevgeni Primakov, Who Pulled Russia Back from the Brink, Has Died

by Rachel Douglas

June 26—Academician Yevgeni Maximovich Primakov, Russia's foremost Arabist, former director of the Russian Academy of Sciences Institute of Oriental Studies, head of the Russian Foreign Intelligence Service, Foreign Minister, Prime Minister, and chairman of the Chamber of Commerce and Industry (CCI), died today at the age of 85, after a two-year battle with cancer. He continued to contribute to Russia's national policy deliberations until very recently, presenting a paper in April at a session of his CCI Mercury Club, titled "Four Errors in Our Economic Policy."

While Primakov had a distinguished career as a specialist in Middle East policy, and knew British and U.S. intelligence operations in that region intimately, being an intelligence operative himself, he was also a leading economist, and his crowning achievement came in government, at the end of the first, disastrous post-Soviet decade in Russia. Appointed prime minister by President Boris Yeltsin after Russia's government bond default of August 1998 (reportedly because industry specialist Yuri Maslyukov refused to accept that office, but said he would serve as deputy PM in a Primakov government—as he then did), Primakov in his eight months in office halted the headlong demolition of Russian industry.

As recounted in the *EIR* Special Report *The New Silk Road Becomes the World Land-Bridge*, "The results of the Primakov-Maslyukov government's measures to salvage Russia's real economy were inherited by Vladimir Putin.... They created a framework, in which decisions in favor of Eurasian continental development might be seriously considered."

"Also of strategic importance," the *EIR* Special Report recalled, "was the outstanding diplomatic en-gagement of this government: Primakov's December 1998 visit to India, during which he proposed the formation of a 'strategic triangle' among Russia, India, and China. The collaboration of these Eurasian powers subsequently came to life through a years-long sequence of three-way academic and diplomatic meetings; after many turns in the road, the 'RIC' combination today is the core of the alliance called the BRICS."

Appreciations of Primakov, cast in precisely these terms, poured in today. Analyst Kirill Benediktov, in a commentary for *Izvestia*, wrote, "Primakov's idea of creating a Great Triangle, Moscow-Delhi-Beijing, is becoming a real political construct before our very eyes, no matter how loud the liberal jackals may yap. Yevgeni Maximovich first proclaimed the idea of the Great Triangle during his visit to Delhi in 1998. Many of us recall the condition Russia was in at that time: politically and economically crushed, having barely survived the August default, and just barely beginning to find our way out of the deep crisis into which Russia had been plunged by the 'young reformers' in alliance with the corrupt members of the Yeltsin Family. And here was the new prime minister of a country which, everybody believed, if it did recover from the misfortunes piled upon it, would not do so any time soon, proposing to his partners in India and China to form a strategic triangle, Moscow-Delhi-Beijing. ... Just seven years after Primakov's visit to Delhi, China and India were already calling themselves 'good neighbors and friends,' and in 2012 Beijing announced that Chinese-Indian relations could become the most important bilateral partnership of the century. And after Russia's 'isolation' by the Atlantic West, it became apparent that Moscow's joining the alliance of great Eurasian nations, as it took shape, was the only pathway to preservation of its political and economic sovereignty."

President Putin and Foreign Minister Lavrov were among those issuing statements of appreciation today for the life and unending work of Primakov, who will be buried June 29 at Moscow's Novodevichy Cemetery.

The Satanic Force of the British Monarchy Can and Must Be Destroyed

Lyndon LaRouche held the following discussion with LaRouche PAC activists by telephone on June 25. John Ascher moderated the call. The audio is available. In response to Ascher's question about opening remarks, LaRouche presented his statement, made earlier that day, on the Greek crisis.

LaRouche on the Greek Crisis: The Only Way Out of This Mess

June 25—The European Union is just stalling, economist Lyndon LaRouche said today. That should be said. They're just stalling. They know what the issues are, and the Greeks have made it clear that the issues are limited, so cut that crap out. Because otherwise, if they're not going to do that, then just call it off and move the Greeks off into a different department, and they'll leave Europe. That's the only way to put it. Say, either you guys get reasonable, and stop trying to stretch out all these things,—the only thing to do is to make a statement.

Say, the problem here, in this discussion, is that some parts of Europe are refusing to admit the fact that their governments, or their representatives, have committed a fraud against the Greek people. And those elements are demanding that they get consideration: that the Greeks have to pay the debt, which is a fraud that has been created. Just simply say that the fraud will not be honored.

You stole the money, for pure speculation, and you're now demanding to get it all over again. And we're saying, "No. You've stolen more than enough from us already." That should be the slogan.

The fly in the ointment is, that an honest treatment of the debts which are attributed to the Greeks, would mean that we would be bankrupting major speculative interests in Europe and the United States, in particular. Therefore, the only way to settle this thing, is not to worry about what the Greeks are doing. The problem that Europe has to worry about, is the fact that the European debts, which are these gambling debts, are not fungible. Therefore, this would mean, for example, cancelling Wall Street, and going back to Glass-Steagall.

We should be saying, "You guys miss the point. Because what you're defending, are worthless assets. You're trying to recommit a fraud, which you had already committed previously. Now, cut it out: what you have to do, is go to a global Glass-Steagall policy. Come along with the United States, and we'll restore the Glass-Steagall policy in the United States. And we'll cancel the worthless debts. And you, in Europe, you will cancel your worthless debts of the same nature. Especially the British." And that's the only way to handle this.

The fact is that the only way that this is going to work: the Europeans must eat, what they should eat. Because we know that much of their banking sector is purely speculation. And what they're demanding, is the protection of their thievery, in effect. The solution is the re-establishment of the Glass-Steagall policy for the relevant regions of the planet, including the U.S.A., and so forth and so on. We'll all go back to a Glass-Steagall policy.

eu

Greek Prime Minister Alexis Tsipras (far right) at his June 22 confrontation with the EU swindlers: from the left, Christine Lagarde, Managing Director of the IMF; Jean-Claude Juncker, President of the European Commission; Mario Draghi, President of the European Central Bank; and French President François Hollande.

That's the only way to get out of this mess, because if you close down the banks in the U.S. which are speculative banks, you do it under U.S. law. And therefore, you have now changed the character of the money system in the United States, in particular, to eliminate this swindle system. You return to Glass-Steagall. Now you use the fact that you went back to Glass-Steagall, to use that as a source of credit. You put that source of credit into the hands of the U.S. government, so it's now the U.S. government, which is the agency which represents the people of the United States. We recommend that a similar approach be applied to Germany, to France, and so forth. In that way, yes, the swindlers lose the money. But the swindlers are swindlers. So what we do, is we take the swindlers' money away from them, and give it back, respectively, to national banks, that is to governmental banking systems. And we create a new Glass-Steagall policy of international development in a significant part of the trans-Atlantic region. That's the one thing we must throw on the table.

Now, you just imagine German Finance Minister Schäuble and so forth, all these creeps, pirates and burglars, are out squawking to protect the so-called interest of the pirates and swindlers. Let's go back to Franklin Roosevelt methods; and Franklin Roosevelt's method is the model. France needs it. Trying to swindle Greece is not going to help France one bit. What you want to do is have a cleanup of the situation; to clean up the monetarist system. That will not solve all problems, but it

will give us a foundation from which to build up solutions. Get some production going. And we shut down this euro speculation system; these guys are all thieves. And the British most of all. So, we don't need to worry about their benefits; they don't have any benefits coming to them.

What we need is an economic system, a Federal banking system, a national banking system. You need to clean the whole thing up and go back to the U.S. concept of Franklin Roosevelt, of Glass-Steagall. The point is, that it's the swindler class which is making these demands of Greece. Don't listen to the swindlers; go back to national economy, and we won't have such swindlers.

Ascher: All right, Lyn. We'll now begin the questions.

No Mystery: It's the British Empire!

Q: My name is L— from New York City. I particularly wanted to call attention to the effort behind the release of the 28 pages that is happening at the legislative level in Congress. I'm sure many on the call are aware of H.Res. 14 and S. 1471 in the Senate. And there's great potential here to begin to unravel the official version of 9/11, which will in turn unravel so much of what's behind the international globalist power structure, controlling events and forcing their agenda through, for instance, the passage of the TPP in the Senate recently, despite public opposition and so forth.

Reuters/Saudi Press Agency/Handout

The evil team: Saudi Prince Bandar bin Sultan (right) welcomes former British Prime Minister Tony Blair to Jeddah, September 3, 2007. Bandar was ambassador to the U.S. at the time of 9/11.

And, it's very necessary that we mobilize large numbers of people to support the brave legislators who have taken the initiative on this through their legislation, again H.Res. 14 and S. 1471.

And there's great potential here, but we need to create a massive groundswell, because they need help, they need the public to urge, put pressure on all the other legislators around the country to, one, read the 28 pages, which they have security clearance for; and that alone will cause a major awakening to the falsehoods behind 9/11. And then [end] the ensuing chaos in terms of our military policy, and the upheaval in the Middle East and the entire fraudulent agenda, particularly when it comes to the clash of civilizations that we're seeing in the world.

LaRouche: I think I have something to add on this. The subject area you presented in your statement just now, is, of course, fully valid. I have no problem with that. Remember I was watching what was happening in New York City at the time the two planes destroyed much of New York City, and killed a lot of New York citizens.

Now, I'm aware of what that was. I have a lot of background on knowing what this is about. I know who did it. I know it was the British Monarchy, together with Saudi Kingdom. It was mostly Saudi agents, who actually delivered that assassination, particularly in the emphasis of New York City as a target.

Now, therefore, the question is, what's important? What is it? What is the so-called secret? If the fact is known, and I've known it before it was generally told

because I was working against this problem, and it just hit me when I was watching New York, as practically a reporter, and I walked through it step by step. I saw each step, I saw each of the two towers coming down; I personally saw that, as an observer!

So there is no mystery. I also know that the Saudis were the ones who did the bombing. It was the Saudis. It was the chief Saudi at the time, also at the same time a representative to the United States by the Saudi Kingdom. The British created the whole process. The whole history of that, is that.

The problem has been, that someone says, "Well, you don't know the secret pages." I say, "What're you talking about? What difference does it make?" We know what happened and we know who did it. And we know who the culpable people are in both the present term, the Bush Administration and the Obama Administration: They both covered up the truth! They both concealed a massive attack on the United States, and they're talking about this and that, and so forth and so what. It's fake. And at that time, when I was functioning at various ways internationally, through my own work in operating in Europe, operating in Russia sometimes, operating in other parts of the world, operating with Britain, where certain interests in Britain were interested in preventing what was being produced at that time; not all British are evil; not even all British officials are evil.

So it was British Empire-concocted, Saudi operation—the *Saudi Kingdom*, which is a satellite of the British Empire, and *they did it*. Now, you have people in the United States, who were senators and other members of Congress; and they say you can't know what the story is. But I already knew it before the story was delivered. I didn't have to have any number of pages to know what had been done. I already had the information *before* that question of the 28 pages came up.

The point is, asking for help from the United States government, under the Bush or the Obama administration, or both, is an exercise in futility, a tragic exercise in futility. What do you have to do? You have to remove those elements of government, including from the Congress, including from members of the Houses and so forth, you have to pull the chain on them.

The Bush Administration, under the control of Cheney, who was the real thug in this matter—he was pretty much a thug in all kinds of matters; but, Obama. Obama is a lying thug. And the shame of the United States today, is that Obama is still treated as President.

He should have been dumped out of there a long time ago. He has no characteristics of any good that qualify him as a President.

Therefore, yes, your concern is valid. But the point is, if we're going to win the fight to correct this terror, we're going to have to go at the real issue, the real *facts*. Whether you have access to certain numbers of pages from a reading from the United States administration's creation of this record, that is not the fundamental question. The fundamental question is, even without those pages, we already know who did what to whom. We don't know some of the details, but we know enough to draw an absolute conclusion on what the truth of this matter is.

What you're saying, your point as argument is absolutely correct. *But!* you have a right, also, to get the full information, not the question of so many pages. The evidence was already presented *to my personal knowledge* in a significant degree, and to people with whom I collaborated in a broader degree, in a circumstance where I had done advanced work, as a specialist investigating the British Empire and its relationship to the Saudis. I had a track on it. I didn't have the exact dates and so forth of this thing, but I had the evidence. I knew the things and I knew the party that took the planes out of Boston, and brought the two towers down. I watched that! And I followed up on that, from Boston and so forth.

I don't have all the facts, but I have enough facts to prove the case, with a lot of details put to one side. And the people in the Federal government, in the *agencies* of the security agencies of the U.S. government, have access to this story. They're committing a fraud. So those institutions which are supposed to be our security institutions ain't very good at protecting the security of the people of the United States. Not when it comes to Obama, or when it comes to Bush, or it comes to Cheney.

Restoring Sovereignty

Q: Hello, Mr. LaRouche. My name's J—. I'm from White Plains, New York. In laymen's terms, can you tell us, does the passage of the Trans-Pacific Partnership trade deal, also known as Obamatrade, will it have a devastating blow on America's sovereignty? And also, does it threaten the BRICS nations? Thank you.

LaRouche:: Both are true. But I would think what Obama has done in particular—remember, he's made two swipes at this thing—what he's done particularly, is

actually a mortal threat to great numbers of American citizens. Because he's going to deprive them of necessary health care in terms of medications.

Remember, the whole thing has included the control of medications on the international market. What this means is that more people are going to die at a more fast rate than ever before, unless Obama is thrown out of the Presidency; that's what's going to happen. That really is the short term of the thing; I can give you more if you want, but that's the short term.

Q: This is D—. I'm in Indianapolis, Indiana. Good evening, Mr. LaRouche and thank you for having these Fireside Talks. What I wanted to ask you to clarify is the difference between Hamilton's National Bank and the Federal Reserve Bank; because some people are confusing it, thinking that what Hamilton was calling for is another Federal Reserve.

LaRouche:: It's not really that. There are elements of the Federal Reserve design which have gone through a lot of changes over the period of more than a century now. There are aspects to that. But if you look at it from the standpoint of what Hamilton's record was, that Hamilton was associated closely, in his leading position in the United States, with George Washington... He was the key advisor and designer of the U.S. economic system, the foundations of it: He did it. He did it with the cooperation of two other members of the body which conducted the Congressional proceedings which created the United States.

Now, there's another side which is very, very ugly. We had, after the death of George Washington, and after the fisherman from New York State [John Adams], who was a good man, but not really competent beyond what he did in France. He did some excellent work on behalf of the United States in France. But after that, for 20 years at least, there was not a decent president in the United States, not a President who was not a crook, and implicitly a traitor to the United States.

Then we get to a great President [John Quincy Adams], who had one term at that point. Then we have Abraham Lincoln; then we have the great general [Grant] who commanded the forces against the Confederacy, and we had another President at the beginning of the Twentieth century, who was assassinated—as many Presidents of the United States have been assassinated, by people who share the same opinions as many in the South did, the Confederacy.

Then we had Franklin Roosevelt, a great man who was assigned to four terms in office; he did not live out

EIRNS/Stuart Lewis

Alexander Hamilton's statue in front of the U.S. Treasury Building. A sculpture by James Earl Fraser.

all four terms. Immediately after that, we had the FBI, and the FBI and Truman destroyed much of the work of the United States under Roosevelt. And we had a very evil system.

Then we had a President [Eisenhower] who was very good, but he was not really effective in trying to deal with the danger from within. Then we had another set: We had the Kennedys. One lived for a while as a President, and the other was a Presidential candidate and possible President. Both were assassinated. I had also experience in this; I worked on behalf of the Reagan Administration. It was a subordinate position which I had under the intelligence section of that administration. I negotiated deals with Russia and so forth, some of which were turned around the other way.

And then the Bushes came in. And the Bush family has been the greatest threat, as the constant threat to the United States, ever since that time. And Obama is nothing but a copy of the same thing. The Bush family,

Cheney, so forth; Cheney was evil, probably still is evil. And so we have had a problem with our Presidency. And what was represented at the start, was a great start.

The root, the economic principles of Alexander Hamilton, are still the only competent foundation principles for the United States today. But unfortunately a lot of that has not been observed. Franklin Roosevelt was typical among those who did understand, more or less fully, the details of the great design which was done by Alexander Hamilton, which gave the United States, uniquely, the kind of constitutional powers that the United States was intended to have had under George Washington.

Reversing Injustice

Q: My name is D— and I'm from East Orange, New Jersey. And I was told that you cannot answer personal questions, but I am being cheated by the government. The bank will not send me my full pension check, and I just want to ask LaRouche what he thinks. What can I do? I've written to them three times, and they won't send me my full pension check, for a full 42 years. And I just wanted to know if there's anything he can do to help?

LaRouche:: I think we have a possibility of help. What I mean by that is that, under the present government, particularly the two Bush governments, together with Cheney, and also with Obama—these governments, these presidents, have been the greatest source of oppression and corruption in the history of the United States, other than the Confederacy itself. Their intention is rotten; you see it from the practice, for example, of the two Bush administrations I just referenced, and of the Obama Administration which is now closing into its second term of office. Evil! Absolutely evil!

And we have done nothing about it. What happens every time we get a bunch of people in Congress,— many of our people have essentially pretty good credentials, but they don't always have the courage to carry them out. And that just happened recently on this question of trade bill. We had the majority against Obama, and then another step was made, and they shut it down, practically. Or tried to shut it down so far.

So you were cheated again! Not an uncommon thing in U.S. history in modern times. Therefore, we're always in the process of fighting on these issues. The problem is to get people on two points; that is, the ordinary citizens. Remember the ordinary citizen knows, as you must understand this as well as other people do, that government in the United States today is rarely fair; that politics and political favors, and political solutions and so forth, come first, and justice to the citizen occurs, occasionally, but it's not reliable. You cannot guarantee that it's going to be delivered to you the next time around.

What we do need, of course, is a Presidency. Now, I would say, there's one thing that's missing, and it's not really mentioned enough: Glass-Steagall. Under Franklin Roosevelt, we achieved the greatest improvement in the design of our governmental system that we have had up to the present time. John F. Kennedy was actually a hero in that direction. There are other cases like that, as great individuals, or even Presidents I've known personally who were good people, but were not given the power, to exercise the good that needed to be done, often very urgently.

So that's where we are. Now, we're at a point now where we're on the edge of the threat of the virtual extinction of the human species. And so all these kinds of injustices and evils which we have experienced in past times, are now coming down to becoming really almost a genocide, a general genocide, a mass killing of human species. That's what's been threatened.

There's now something from Britain that's come out trying to turn the Popes into becoming murderers—you know, this is the kind of the thing that's going on right now, under the Obama Administration, for example. So therefore, all I can say, and guarantee in what you're asking about, which I consider a very fair question, is, how do we get the job done?

And I think we can, possibly, actually win the fight on this case: The threat to humanity is almost universal. That is, there are forces in Europe and elsewhere, which are determined to—oh, Obama, for example. If Obama were to carry out his current military policy, there would not be much of anyone living on the planet Earth. Because any war which Obama would start now, would be a terminal war. That is, in a strategic sense, the kind of thermonuclear warfare which Obama is insisting on producing, and it's Obama himself who's doing it. Actually the Queen of England is the real evil, but Obama takes the point, because he's the President.

And the danger is, we're not going to exist any more, unless we can do something. For example, if Obama were removed from office now, I think that the result would be that we would not have a thermonuclear war. But the way he's going now, and he's acting like a maniac, just completely irresponsible, and acting like

White House/Eric Draper

Cheaters in the Presidency: Here, President George W. Bush and Vice President Dick Cheney on August 14, 2006.

an idiot. And that's dangerous.

All he has to do, and he's got the figures inside his Administration to do it, is to set into force a thermonuclear war, which, if the United States were to start it, would be responded to by Russia and other nations, and the result would be, there's no security in the hope that maybe humanity would survive.

So that's what we're living up against. And what you're talking about is perfectly legitimate. It's an essential element of the kind of problem, the kind of threats, under which our citizens live. But beyond that, there's something much more menacing: There's a threat of the extinction of the human species, which could come as soon as this summer, and that's what we have to stop.

Obama Means War

Q: My name's D— and I'm from California. I have a two-part question—a statement and then a question, but I wanted to preface this with: I think your leadership is great, first of all, with the BRICS and everything, but my concern is when you're going up against world powers and establishments that have been there a long time, wouldn't it be a more effective or authoritative to have the identity of the United States in terms of the three branches of government behind you, in terms of like a Presidency, or something like that?

LaRouche:: I got it. I got it; it's a question which people often ask, and therefore in that degree is legitimate. For me to say something like that would not be legitimate because I know better.

I have a certain kind of expertise in these matters. No, what we're on the edge of right now, is a general

NATO

NATO's Rapid Reaction Corps training in 2014. On June 24, NATO decided to triple its size, from 13,000 to 40,000.

thermonuclear war. Now, if Obama pushes Russia—Russia will not start a war, that's very clear. Anyone who understands this thing knows Russia does not intend to start a war. Russia intends to discourage threats, from attacking Russia and from attacking others.

If such a war were launched, it would not come from Russia; it would come from the British Empire, and from stooges of the British Empire, such as Obama. And Obama is an enthusiast for this thing; the great danger now is the fact that the Obama Presidency, right now, is the most likely trigger for setting off a thermonuclear war, which would occur with a launching *by* Obama and his advisors.

And the United States and Britain are the only nations which have that kind of commitment right now. Other nations have all their problems and all these kinds of things.

So the issue is, to prevent the Obama Administration from going ahead with his advisors to launch an attack on Russia. If that were to occur, you would have a global thermonuclear war in immediate chain-reaction, and the question is, would anything survive? This is the most insane thing that man could ever do. It's the ultimate expression of insanity for mankind. Now that doesn't mean that somebody might not survive, but I don't think there will be survivors to tell the story, if at all.

And so, the issue has to be taken seriously: We cannot compromise. When you have a nut like Obama, and the people who are behind him from the British royalty who are really his masters, you're not dealing with something you can negotiate with. You can either weaken his power, or take his power away from him, or take the dangerous toys away from this idiot, hmm? this fanatical idiot.

And otherwise, I tell you, it is not unreasonable to presume, that if Obama is not removed from office, there might not be a human race over the course of this summer. That's the fact, the actual fact of the matter. And everybody who understands what thermonuclear war means, understands exactly what I just said.

Q: B—, who is listening on YouTube, submitted the following question: "Concerning all the Executive Orders Obama has signed, aren't they illegal? In my opinion, we need to clean house from the top to the bottom, and this President has been a complete failure from the word go. It's time to get him out, along with Biden. We are in a very bad situation here. It's time for the world to know who Obama works for, period."

LaRouche: Well, I think that's a real fact; that's the truth. We do have to.

Now, we're not totally impotent in this matter, but the threat is so great, that we have to realize that what we're doing is, we're dealing with a potential ultimate danger. And we have to define what the ultimate danger is, if it is a reasonably serious danger. And what I've said, for example, about what Obama's policy is in terms of his relationship to his master or mistress, the Queen of England, is serious. It is deadly.

You also have a thing which got into the British System in the name of the Papacy, which is to reduce the population of the United States, or the world as a whole, in fact, from the present population level, to less than one billion people. And do it quickly by mass starvation.

The policy, to create that effect, is already in place. It's been announced in the recent couple of weeks. It was presented clearly. The danger is very great.

Now what you can do to get sort of a solution, a closure on this thing, is to recognize those who would—and that's the Queen of England, essentially, that's the leadership—assassinate the majority of the human population, reduce it from the present population, down to about one billion people, at most. That is sort of the same thing as what I've been talking about in terms of the war danger. It's a different aspect, but it goes to the same kind of intention.

That's where we are. We have to change the world in a way which is not unreasonable in any sense. We have to do the things we call the good things.

Let me add one thing. Why is it that, in fact, as I know the facts, since the end of the Nineteenth Century, the beginning of the Twentieth Century, as with the case of some evil characters up there, we have been moving, in the United States, in Britain and elsewhere, in a long-term tendency to reduce the conditions of life of mankind, in the United States and beyond? Around the world generally.

Yes, we've made some progress, particular progress. But if you look at the conditions of life of the typical American citizen, since the beginning of the Twentieth Century to the present time, the condition of life of the average citizen of the United States has been degenerating. And when you look at it in the long term, up to the present date, from the beginning of the Twentieth Century, you see that everything is threatening everybody. Employment. Conditions of life. Education. All of the things we used to take for granted, back in the earlier part of the Twentieth Century, are now being taken away.

The death rate is increasing, the corruption, the destitution is increasing. And it tends to be that way throughout the United States, and throughout much of Europe.

Other parts of the planet, like South America, are improving now, in terms of its conditions, or some of South America. China has made a tremendous success. It's become the most important nation on the planet right now, in terms of its power, its capabilities, its rate of growth. Other parts of the world, in Asia, some parts

James Rea
Twentieth Century degeneration in action: A rock concert in Germany, June 2010.

of Asia, some parts of South America, are improving.

But for us in the United States, and for us in Europe itself, we are all actually falling into an absolute disaster. And if you can think back to what the conditions were at the beginning of the Twentieth Century, as I came in closely after the Twentieth Century, things were then much better. Things were going in a much better direction. Yes, there were many problems, many problems which preceded the First World War, and which continued after that. But the real bad stuff came about 1980, and after 1980, into the middle of the 1980s, then we began to go—in the United States—down toward Hell, step by step by step by step.

And we've got to change it.

Q7: I'm C— in Apple Valley. My concern is this, Mr. LaRouche: I was just reading where President Obama had just initiated an Executive Order number 13603, where he authorizes slave labor on a large scale, on American soil. And another thing is, the FEMA camps that they've got through this JM15. And I don't know when they're going to start rounding up Americans, because I know one thing: If we wind up in a FEMA camp, we're not getting out of there. I've heard people say, whatever you do, don't let them catch you alive.

So, where do we stand on that aspect?

LaRouche: Well, I think it's up to us to come back to our senses. We really do have the potential ability, as an American citizenry, to cure many of these great threats, and other kinds of conditions. But we don't do it. The reason is, that we look at the other guy as being the responsible person to get us out of this trouble we might be facing.

What people say is, they use the word "They." "They" don't let us do this. "They" don't do this for us. Huh?

Their attitude is that they do not take responsibility for what happens to the people who live under our government. They always want to say, "they." "Well, I'm not ready to act because I'm not ready to act to deal with this problem. I'm not going to take a risk to deal with this problem. I'm not going to solve the problem? So, they go along. They pass the buck.

They say: "I've got a problem. Somebody has to help me."

Well, that's fine; we'll try to help you. But, will you try to help yourself, too? That's the issue. And then if you do want to help yourself, don't you have to find out what the skills are you need to adapt, to do that? Don't you have to discover what the facts are that you have to take into consideration, to deal with the threat to you, and to your family, and to the nation?

And the problem is, many people just don't have the guts to step up and show leadership, when the public as a whole needs leadership.

I know this very well. I think many of you out there know that just as well: that people duck the issue. They don't take responsibility. Shall we say, they don't make good soldiers? They always go out in the latrine and hide, when the battle is about to begin. I think we should cure that. I think we should take that seriously.

History: The Deep Roots of Crisis

Q: We have a question from Professor Francis Boyle from the University of Illinois Law School, on the danger of World War III. He says: "I wish to give my personal regards to both Lyndon and Helga LaRouche. We are in a very, very serious and nearly cataclysmic situation with regard to Russia over Ukraine, as well as the disintegrating situation currently in the Middle East, which also threatens to pull in Russia, as well as Iran. Obama is also threatening war with China as well. Clearly World War III could break out very soon, at any time, if Obama keeps moving in this direction. It seems to me, like all of these so-called political conflicts, including the cultural warfare we are now witnessing here at home, have been deliberately designed to distract public attention away from the buildup towards World War III abroad.

"Can you shed some light on this imminent danger, and what the citizens of our republic have a responsibility to do, given the proximity of this danger, and the

NATO

U.S. Secretary of Defense Ashton Carter at his June 25 press conference at NATO headquarters, announcing further deployment of military hardware on Russia's borders.

lateness of the hour, for the very survival of civilization?"

LaRouche: Okay, good. The question is the practical problem that is presented. If you want to go through the details, it can be a very long story, because it's a story of history. It's not a story of what might have happened yesterday; but it's a story of what might have happened in the course of history. And the course of history is sometimes very deep. It accumulates; the course of history accumulates. Sometimes it goes in a better direction; the danger is moved away. And then sometimes it comes back, or it comes with a new fresh surge.

What we have now, is, first of all, we have idiots, and we have unintentional but effective murderers. They don't intend to kill people, but they will kill people, and they will stubbornly cling to the actions which will result in killing people. And that's not just killing people.

Because we're dealing with a gentleman whose powers of reason are well-known to me, in responding to this question, I want to give a fair expression to a more than fairly competent personality.

There are underlying mistakes, which have often been made in history, which are little understood. What we do tend to understand, are things which our accumulated experience shows us are threatening us. That's what happens. People see the coming of a war;

they become uncertain, and so forth. But they don't necessarily find the answer in time, because they don't look at the depths of the problem they're dealing with. They want to ignore it up until the time that they got scared, and that frightens them. And that's what we see.

Therefore, what happened in our history of our Presidency, for example. We had a great President, who had one of the most brilliant minds in the world, today, still, who was the official leader and guide of that great President Washington—Hamilton. Hamilton was the great genius, who made the United States accession possible, as opposed to those who—despite George Washington—turned against Hamilton, and killed him, and intended to kill him. We had Presidents in that period who actually were enemies of the institution of the United States, even among the early Presidencies.

THE ASSASSINATION OF PRESIDENT LINCOLN.
AT FORD'S THEATRE WASHINGTON D.C APRIL 14TH 1865.

Library of Congress

We have to look at the deeper issues of history, LaRouche said—for example, the history of the Presidency.

So, we have to often look at the deeper issues, in order to come to a competent understanding of what the crisis is, which may threaten us in a recent time.

People find, at the time that they wake up, it's often much too late. And I think that he knows what I mean by that. He's had enough experience and study to know that.

Now, there are certain things I do know, and I do know what this stuff's about: it's my specialty; that's why I know it. But we are at the point, where we could be extinct within a matter of weeks. I'm not exaggerating at all. Just take, for example, the situation of Russia vis-à-vis the United States, with the United States and Britain controlling a threatened war with Russia.

The war would not come from Russia. Some of the shooting might come quickly, the minute that Putin were to act to recognize that the Obama administration and its British associates, are prepared to launch a general thermonuclear war against the United States—really, it's against the United States, but it's against Europe, in general—the war is on. And if it happens sometime in the early summer, which is a likely time… Everything is now building up very closely to the point

of a ripeness for a general thermonuclear war; and when that general thermonuclear war occurs, on the next day, there will be a lot of people who suddenly went out of existence on this planet.

That's the effect.

Therefore, we have to understand this issue, and we have to operate on that basis. People who are trying to say, how do we get rid of this thing, conquer this guy, beat this guy; how do we start this war, suppress that—these people are just worse than fools. Because we're at a point where the potential that the mankind has built into himself, into man's culture, especially into a trans-Atlantic period, has created an intention for thermonuclear warfare, whether they know it or not.

And the Administration of Obama *knows* it. The Administration of Obama, that is, Obama himself, *knows* it. So if a war is going to break out, it's going to break out, probably, because of Obama. Because Obama is able, like others who might be involved in this, to take a step which moves Russia to a thermonuclear action, and at that moment, the general extinction of humanity on much of this planet will occur within *a very, very short time.*

Therefore, what we have to do, knowing this fact, the fact of the threat of thermonuclear war right now, in those terms,—you know that in a matter of the summer weeks, we are now approaching the point where the interaction, the frictional processes, could lead to a thermonuclear conclusion, and it could come, right now, it will come from the paws of Obama. He's only a tool, but that's the bomb.

To understand that, demands that we understand what the conditions were that allowed this threat to emerge, as it did not emerge, say, for example, when Bill Clinton was President. There was no such threat, when Bill Clinton was President. Since the Obama period, especially since the Bush family, or since Cheney, you've seen the march toward Hell in process.

If we want to talk about other nations, you can talk about them. But I think the thing which is ours, which is the United States, *we* of the United States must take the responsibility to make sure that forces of the United States are not used for the purposes of the extinction of the human species.

Q: This is R— from Brooklyn. One of the factors that I discussed at one meeting, was that Obama put the 173rd Airborne and the Screaming Eagles as advisors in Kiev. And that's a highly unstable thing that he did. Is there any way that we can undo some of this, even though his Administration may still be in power?

LaRouche: I would say the only thing at this point, which gives you much chance, is impeaching Obama, throw him out of office. I'm talking about what I see in actions around the Congress. I follow somewhat the decisions of the U.S. government, or at least some of the things that are most attracted to my attention. And I would say, if we could throw Obama out of office, in the right way, right now, we could probably prevent World War—Four, Five, and Six, and so forth.

If we can't do that, we're in real deep trouble. And so everyone says, we're on the side of the United States. What do you mean, you're on the side of the United States? We're talking about thermonuclear war. Hey buddy, you're the guy who's going to get fried. And all your friends will be fried, too. And it will be done quickly, and you will not be able to do a damned thing about it.

That's the issue. The question is, how do we mobilize the forces? I think, as I just mentioned in response to a friend of ours, that you have to look at the deep roots of any threat of this nature. The deep roots. The deep historical roots. They sometimes go back to decades, or even longer.

Most people don't have any knowledge of what history is. They may sometimes be able to get a chronology, and say that at this point this happened, at this point this happened, at this point this happened—but they don't understand what the process was. They don't understand what the *causes* of the process were. They don't know how you change the causes, that lead into something which is good, or something which is bad.

And so most people are left ignorant. They have no knowledge of what this process is. They're a little bit like victims, living on the assumption of hope, when they lack knowledge. And therefore, often, mankind has gone from brilliant periods of history, as with Nicholas of Cusa, and people like that—and then what happened later? They suddenly have the outburst of one of the most wicked and evil wars, fought as religious wars, in that period, into the time of Leibniz, and beyond.

And what happened when Leibniz died? We had the underlying [idea] of the United States, the future United States, reversed. And a stroke of evil struck what was becoming the United States, the future United States, and we had presidents who were rotten. The first three Presidents of the United States [after Washington] were rotten—most people don't know that, but that's the case.

Therefore, the issue here is, we have to understand the deep roots of the great movements in human history. We have to understand what our relationship is to those great roots, and most people don't. They haven't been educated. Or they've been conditioned to accept indifference, or to assume that everything is confused until some short-term development occurs. Or an accident occurs. One of the favorite fantasies of people is accidents, fatal accidents included. Automobile accidents, other kinds of accidents.

The issue is, yes, those things do happen, but what are we doing in anticipation of the fact that they *might* happen? How might they be prevented? How may poisoning be prevented? How may the accidents be reduced? All these kinds of things. And I think the point is that mankind is poorly educated these days. It's not because of the individual as such; it's because of society, which no longer gives much care for members of society.

And a few of us, who had our hide torn up a bit, do understand these things, because we've had the experience; we know what happens. And other people hope that they don't have to know what's going to happen.

Smithsonian Institution, National Museum of American History, Archives Center

What we have lost: Marian Anderson singing at the Lincoln Memorial in Washington, D.C., April 9, 1939.

Tyranny and Treason

Q: This is K— from Massachusetts. About our humanity, and it states in the Constitution that—of course, you just don't do it for any old reason, but if you're under like a tyranny, the citizens have the right to get rid of that tyranny, get it out. And I don't understand why we're not doing that.

LaRouche: What do you mean by right?

Q: In other words, it states that if you have an overbearing government, that the citizens have the right to get rid of that overbearing government, and get a new government. For example, as you were explaining, Mr. LaRouche, about setting up a new Presidency now.

LaRouche: Oh, great, great! I think we could probably improvise one right away, if somebody would politely and kindly supply us with a replacement to Obama. Frankly, that's it. If we could get a President who comes in, stumbling as he or she may be, at least if they stumbled around and it leads to some kind of reasonable—like, does the person know how to drive an automobile? He or she may not be the best driver in the world, but if he or she intends to avoid contusions and so forth, they might be preferred over the madman who is a reckless driver.

I think, in general, those considerations are true. But

I would not like to have our citizens dependent upon accidents, successful good accidents.

Q11: Hi, this is K— from Iowa. I was just wondering, what is going on with the 28 pages?

LaRouche: I don't think that those pages, in and of themselves, are going to solve the problem. Because the 28 pages have been around for a long time, and they've been available, as such. But the pages are not, really, the important issue of fact. They're an important issue about the way the whole thing was handled, but they're not the issue in fact. The issue in fact is what I saw, via video, looking at the two planes, successively circling the southern part of Manhattan. And I saw the destruction of those towers, and the killing of the people in and around them. That's what I know is the fact.

Also, as I said earlier, I know some of the facts behind this thing, the facts that are not discussed. Like "Who did it?" Well, I know who did it. It was the Saudis. It was the Saudi forces that did 9/11.

The Saudis are the key agents of the British agency. I knew this before it happened! Because I was following the British operation. I knew the forces in Britain, which were operating out of Saudi Arabia, were the forces which created 9/11. I knew that the official representative of the Saudi Kingdom, in Washington, D.C. was a key element in causing 9/11. I also know a lot of other evidence, which I've received by sharing it on side issues which are related to this, how the thing happened, why it happened, and who did it! I *know* that!

Now, then someone comes along, and says, "What about the pages?" Well, that pages thing is, yes, a true case. But why are the pages suppressed? See? You can't say the pages are the problem. Why are the pages suppressed? The Federal government has them suppressed. The Bush Administration had the evidence. Obama has had the evidence. He has had the evidence that the Saudis, working together with the British, committed the crime against the United States. Why is the United States, then, *hiding* the identity, of the murderers, the mass-murderers, who attacked our citizens in Manhattan, in particular, on that occasion?

That's the issue! And the whole thing's a swindle. You say the 9/11 issue. That is a swindle. It's a fraud; it's a fraud, an act of treason by the Bush Administration. It's an act of treason, as continued by the Obama administration. If you can't say that, you have no credibility. You may know the thing happened, but you have no credibility, which allows you to walk in with the *proof*, that the Bush Administration and the Obama Administration have both been responsible for the effects—the murderous effects, on our citizens in 9/11.

The substitute for reality for huge sections of the U.S. population. Here, some one learns how to download YouTube videos on an iPad Mini.

And therefore, neither Bush, nor Cheney, of course, nor Obama, is actually fit to be President of the United States, and *never was*. That's your problem. If Bush had been removed, for his crime; if Obama had been removed, for perpetrating the conclusion in that same crime; why are they in the Presidency?

Don't ask me about the pages; I know about the pages. I support the people who are trying to force the effort to try and expose the pages, to bring them out, as against those members of Congress, and the White House, who refuse to allow that to be exposed.

I know what happened. I don't know all the details; I may not know some of the delicate details of the pages. But that's not important. The question is, "*Who* did it?" I know who did it. It was the British Empire steering its puppet, the Saudis. That's what the story is. And everything else is a distraction; it's a fraud.

Developing Competence in the Citizenry

Q12: Hello. My name is C— and I'm calling from Maryland. And I just heard about Mr. LaRouche last week, when I met two guys I see, at the MVA in Gaithersburg. And I have a question, though; actually I have two questions.

The first question is: Since we have been looking at the activities of the Presidents, especially, Mr. LaRouche was talking about what President Bush did, and all the activities which have been actually against the

people, and the will of the people, and then just giving it names and all that, and wars, and everything. And I know it's against the people's will. And Obama came into power and he did the same thing.

How do we know, and what guarantee do we have, that the next President, of all these candidates that are campaigning right now, are just not going to carry on with the same sham of a show?

And, the other question that I have is: How would we mobilize the people? Because this is actually a serious threat to the existence of the people. And how would this beautiful act that you are carrying out right now, how is it going to be known to the rest of the people, if we have to mobilize? Because the change actually comes by mobilizing enough people, and then people will act upon the principles being propagated by an organization, such as yours. How would we have to do that? Because, I mean, nowadays people, all they do is watch TV, play games, and go to work. I would do as much as I can, in order to influence my peers, so they can see what's happening, really.

I have friends in China, I have friends in South Africa—I have friends everywhere. And we talk about these things every day, and, you know, we think about what could be done in order to end this madness. But the rest of the people seem rather to be, you know, they're caught up in a wave of dreaming, and just not wanting to do anything. You know what I'm trying to say?

LaRouche: Yeah, I do. Well, the problem is, largely,

that the people in the United States have become increasingly ignorant, among other things. The level of intelligence, on all levels, even scientific intelligence; you know, we had one scientist, serving in the United States, in the Twentieth Century. Now there were other scientists, who were capable people who made contributions. But as to the profound underlying principles of science, Einstein was the one man who qualified for that, Albert Einstein.

We have access, now, to new knowledge, which was not possessed by us in that century, which we know now. We know the solution for the water problem. We don't have the practical solution in hand; but we know what the principle is. We know how we can improve the moisture level, management of the moisture level delivered to mankind, on different parts of the planet. We know these things. We know many other things, which are very useful, as scientists.

But most ordinary people, in terms of education, in terms of experience, have almost *no* knowledge of these matters. And therefore the ignorance of our people— See, the idea of the individual is sometimes exaggerated. You say, "individual opinion"; what about the individual opinion of a person who is totally ignorant? Do you want that as a standard of government? Do you expect that that standard of government will protect the nation against mischances, and terrible effects? No.

Therefore, we depend upon a social process. We're not talking about individuals, so-called "rugged individuals." There are no rugged individuals. There are only successful ones, and unsuccessful ones. There are the ones who are able to do something for mankind, and those who can't.

And our job is to become a part of a group of people who knows how to help people to become competent in their own affairs. I mean, why do people have stupid ideas? Because they're ignorant. Sometimes because they're a thief, and that's their profession; or they're murderers, and that's their profession. But, for most of the time, mankind's problems lie from a lack of intelligence. And the lack of intelligence is that society has failed to provide its young people, and so forth, and older people later, with the kind of knowledge that will give them the ability to *make* competent judgments, to make *competent* judgments.

I'm saying, today, in today's society's moral breakdown, which has gone on over the last half of the Twentieth Century. The Twentieth Century was already a century of decline, in the moral and intellectual quality of mankind. In the last half of the Twentieth Century, the late half, things began to go *down*. And you know, the Bush administrations, the elections of Bushes to Presidencies, is actually a marker of the degeneration of the American people and their population.

The problem is, now—you can't control human behavior by authority. You can try. You may be able to stop some things that shouldn't happen from happening. But, in general, as a policy matter, you have to develop the qualities of creativity, and good judgment in the general population, by good education, by good practice. You're not just supposed to *know* something; you don't really know it unless you can practice it. So, it's not knowing about something, it's knowing how to *do* it; or how you have a friend who can collaborate with you, and do it, have friends who can do it.

So therefore, the question is really one of the development of the human mind. The moral development of the human mind. The scientific development of the human mind. Without those accomplishments, mankind is a dumb animal. Despite all the good means that they may have intended in their own life, within their restrictions of their own judgment, they have been cheated out of the access of the goodness that mankind should be inherently expressing.

A Policy of Evil

Q13: Hi, this is J— and I'm from Orange County. On the note of education, and people staying informed, it is true; people do have to know what's going on in order to make sound judgments.

Not everybody lounges around without staying up-to-date, and reading all the materials that they can get their hands on. . . .

My question was, what about the drought in California, and do we, or you, have any news or any ideas as to what the solution is going to be? Anything would be great.

LaRouche: Okay, I have some expert sources on these subjects. First of all, take the case of the governor of California: He's a bad man, and he's also an ignorant man. He's a bad man because he's actually a murderer. He's saying that the people in California have to be deprived of water, even if it means killing them. That's a bad man. He's the governor of California; his father was a good man. So, it's not the race that's the problem here, it's the lack of brains.

What are we talking about? About goodness and

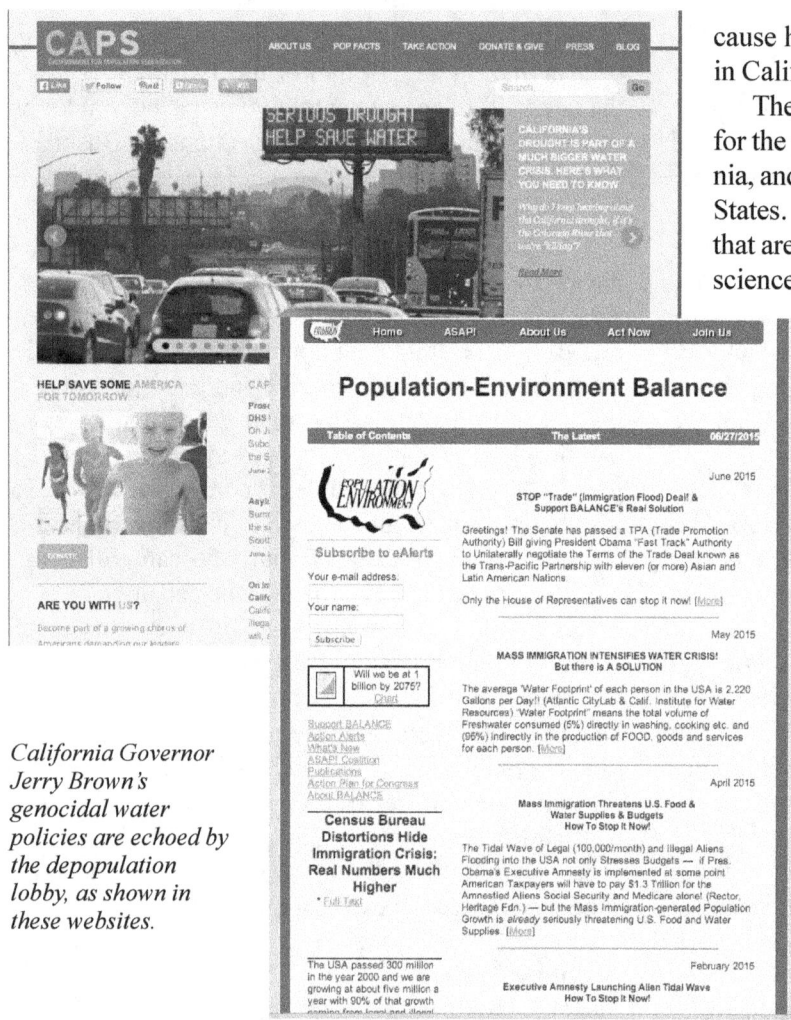

California Governor Jerry Brown's genocidal water policies are echoed by the depopulation lobby, as shown in these websites.

cause he's taking steps to increase the rate of death in California, and there's no need for it!

There is need for supplying the relevant solution, for the problem of the water management in California, and around adjacent parts of the southern United States. Yes, that's needed; there are also other things that are also needed similarly. But mankind, through science, has the access to the ability to understand these things. Kepler discovered the Solar System. No one knew what the Solar System was until Kepler, Johannes Kepler. And, Kepler was followed by Leibniz (and was a follower of Kepler in a scientific sense). Now we have higher development, and we've gone into the higher layer of the whole Galaxy System. And we know some things about the Galaxy System. Not everything. We don't know what the dark areas in the Galaxy System really mean, for example.

But we know these things. We know things about the Moon, for example. We're learning more, China's showing us more things about the Moon. So, we're finding out all kinds of these facts through *scientific exploration*, and study. But so-called practical measures, or rumors, or opinions aren't worth anything, if they're not grounded on something which is tantamount to science. And I know some of these matters, some more indirectly and sometimes directly, and that's the case.

So there is no excuse for the continuation of these problems. There's only the need for the urgency to look into what the solutions are that are available to us. And, like Kepler's discovery of the organization of the Solar System, for example. That was a great discovery, it was unique. He did it! Nobody else did it, until after he'd done it. What we're getting now on the question of the water aspect of the Galactic System: We know that the Galactic System provides most of the Earth's water! And if you don't know how to deal with the Galactic System, that's your mistake.

Without a competent understanding of the meaning of science, it is not possible for us to deal with these problems. *But!* So far, considering the progress of man in science, up to this present time, there is no excuse for the kinds of problems which face us right now on the question of water and other things.

about achievement, these kinds of things? The point is that mankind does have tremendous power in the mind. For example, look at the history of successive modern history. Go from the period of Jeanne d'Arc and so forth, that period, Nicholas of Cusa; great inventors, like Nicholas of Cusa himself; or, like Kepler, or like Leibniz: These were great people. They actually improved man's ability, man's insight into the principles of science; in the broader sense of science, the true sense of science. In the sense of principle, not gimmicks, principle!

What's happened is, we have a supply of water, and the chief supply of water for mankind, is located in the galactic region, not in the next door neighbor. There is no shortage of water for mankind. There is only stupidity by mankind: Because the technology of dealing with the alleged water shortage, is entirely a product of stupidity, or *malicious stupidity*. The governor of California is a malicious mass murderer! The governor! Be-

Evil at play: President Obama holds a discussion with Prince Philip's favorite propagandist for mass murder, Sir David Attenborough, on June 26, 2015.

Ascher: Lyn, I was wondering if you wanted to take a few minutes here to outline some concluding remarks?

LaRouche: Sure, why not? It's a good idea to do it, and it's a fun thing to do. I always enjoy working with our people and our circles of people, because the discussions that we can sometimes get into are profitable for them, and for other people as well. And it does help the process of man's happiness about having fellow-man around someplace.

We're in a gravely endangered period of American history and world history. And what we're seeing recently from around the Pope, actually from the British—the Pope's intention now, or the British intention now—is to reduce the population of the planet to about one-quarter of what the population is today, and to do it rather rapidly. Now this is simply mass-murder, and it's done on the orders of the British Empire, the British Monarchy. It's being done in that phase, and it's being pushed now.

The Pope is being pushed to commit genocide. I mean, this means a reducing of the population, as the stated intention of this action, the intention is to reduce the population of the Earth, permanently. Now, what the effect will be of doing that, would be worse, worse than that, but it's being pushed. It's being pushed chiefly by the British Empire.

To understand what this means, means you have to understand what the British Empire is. Now, let's take the current British Monarchy, including the British Royal Family: These people are on the record as being mass-murderers in the extreme, and as long as the Brit-

ish Empire has any significant power of influence in society, mass-murder in society will spread. It is now spreading rapidly now! Reducing the population of the planet, now, from the immediate size of seven billion people *to one. Mass-murder* of citizens throughout the planet. *And that is what the British Monarchy has as its leading policy*, and it *has* been the leading policy of the British Monarchy, ever since the current British Monarchy came into existence.

That is Satan! The British Monarchy is a Satanic force! And it's the chief force of evil living in the planet today. We're on the verge of an attempted mass-extermination of the human population currently from 7 billion to 1 or less; that's what's on now. And it's the British Monarchy, the Queen herself, her whole shit 'n caboodle. That's what the problem is.

That is the example of what the policy of evil represents in the course of human history during this century, and now.

ICLC Member Charles Hughes, Astronomer, Telescope-Builder

by Dennis H. Speed

June 27—"It is believed that ocean levels were about 400 feet lower during the Ice Age, which lasted for about 100,000 years and began its long melt back about 18,000 years ago. And so, if a city were built on the then-dry continental shelf, which is now under water, that construction or ruin is much older than established science dares admit, in order to hold onto its mistaken axioms concerning human civilization."

So wrote astronomer and tele-scope-builder Charles Hughes in an article that appeared in *21st Century Science & Technology* magazine in the Summer of 2009. Charles, a life-long member of Lyndon LaRouche's International Caucus of Labor Committees (ICLC), and a 45-year political associate of Lyndon LaRouche, died on Sunday, June 21, after a long bout with diabetes, at the age of 77.

In the afore-cited article, Charles had also pointed out that the discovered "cities in the sea" off the coasts of Africa, Asia, the Indian subcontinent and the continental shelves of the Americas were proof that an unknown civilization of sea people was located in the Caribbean, before a time that mainstream establishment science acknowledges that such a civilization existed anywhere in the world. So the science establishment refuses to examine such sites, or reports that they are unusual natural rock formations!

My particular interest has been

the constructions consisting of large walls and docks, made of gigantic stone blocks, and found in the Bahamas on the islands of Andros and Bimini, which were first reported in 1968. It is almost certain that a construction as large as a football field in 20 feet of water on the bottom of

Charles Hughes, with lens for a telescope he built.

Nicholstown harbor, was a quay for loading cargo ships when the area was above sea, in about 8000 B.C.

Hughes, in numerous discussions with both colleagues and newly-interested parties, posed this provocative question: If such cities and areas were "above sea, in around 8000 B.C.", how did they submerge? Such archaeological evidence would seem to demand an "unorthodox," yet rigorous investigation to determine whether the planet has been, in fact, thawing ("warming") over the past nearly 18,000 years, albeit with fluctuation for "little ice ages" prior to the re-commencement of a new 100,000 year "mega" Ice Age, and all without the agency of "anthropocentric, industrial carbon-emissions driven climate change."

Further, if that were the case, might it not be urgent that *vigorous human intervention*, using advanced technologies potentially essential to altering the otherwise inevitable "cyclical trend" of a new Ice Age, destined to appear at the conclusion of the present, waning inter-glacial period, be rapidly pursued, invented, and deployed? Should we, perhaps, not be engaged in a crash program for thermonuclear fusion, and be prepared to massively warm up areas of the planet, such as the Arctic? That was the happy, polemical, "unorthodox" intellectual life of Charles Hughes.

One of Hughes' collaborators in telescope building, Jeremy Batterson, remembered that "he very thoroughly investigated all the details of telescope making, including grinding his own optics. In one case, being low on income, he had bought a glass square, and had the glass company cut off the four corners, leaving him with an octagonal slab of glass. He then created a crude hand machine to grind that octagon down into a circular glass blank, something which alone took months to do. So he *really* started from scratch! His very thorough study on fabrication methods, polishing methods, mounting of blanks during grinding to avoid astigmatism, Foucault tests, and so on, were all carefully taken into account by me."

A 'Renaissance Man'

Hughes, however, was far more. "Charles' active life was a true expression of 'Renaissance man,' as soldier, chemist, metallurgist, geologist, telescope builder, historian, a musical mind. He took such delight in historical Irish-Scottish songs, as well as their companion lieder composed by Beethoven and Haydn," said his friend Cloret Carl Ferguson.

In the 1970s and 1980s, Hughes made his decidedly anti-British, anti-population reduction views very clear in a series of creative, ribald protests against the likes of the notorious New York lawyer Roy Cohn, as well as Henry Kissinger. Kissinger's 1974 National Security Study Memorandum 200, co-produced with then-CIA Director George Bush, was the precursor for the same Malthusian population reduction policies even more rampant today.

Another colleague added that Charles was "a proud pro-Irish, pro-Robbie Burns anti-British oligarchy American patriot. That meant in science as well. He intended that the fraudulent 'anthropocentric global warming' hoax be discredited by precisely the research on ancient civilizations that he both reported and encouraged. Charles believed deeply that 'the world needs more people.' He saw 'climate change' as a sneaky and downright racist attack on Africa, Asia, and South and Central America and the Caribbean. After all, if global warming had commenced 18,000 years ago with the end of the last Ice Age, wouldn't that prove that the industrialization of the past 200 years, and its correlate 'population explosion,' had nothing to do with it?"

Charles' home-made telescope was one of the largest in New Jersey. He sometimes slept on the roof of the office building in Ridgefield Park where he both worked, and had mounted it, "in order to be a little closer to my work." And star-gazer Hughes would have been delighted by the just-released anomaly-filled pictures from the Dawn spacecraft now orbiting the asteroid belt's massive "dwarf planet", Ceres. The new field of asteroseismology, which uses sound waves generated by plasmas that expand and contract high above the surfaces of stars to measure, through "standing waves," changes in their internal composition, providing clues to their evolution, was his idea of "gainful employment" for the human mind.

The last person known to have spoken to him, Margaret Greenspan, said: "He was very special, and I miss him. I spoke to him for the last time on Sunday, and I was told that he called the hospital with chest pains that day, when we were at the big concert at Carnegie Hall. It was Summer Solstice, and also a big solar flare happened that day. There is poetic beauty in that, I think. Charles went out with a flare!"

Every Day Counts In Today's Showdown To Save Civilization

That's why you need *EIR*'s **Daily Alert Service**, a strategic overview compiled with the input of Lyndon LaRouche, and delivered to your email 5 days a week.

Take the example of the ongoing debt showdown with Greece, which now threatens a blowout of the world financial system.

On June 18, *EIR*'s Daily Alert reported that the Greek parliamentary debt commission had issued a report declaring the bailout debt "odious" and "unpayable." On June 22, the Alert reported on an interview by former German Chancellor Helmut Schmidt, where he said the Greek debt was indeed unpayable.

Don't you think you should have known of these developments as they happened? Can you really afford to wait for the consequences?